AVALUE AVERAGING

2nd Edition Revised

VALUE AVERAGING

The Safe and Easy Strategy for Higher Investment Returns

MICHAEL E. EDLESON

International Publishing Corporation
Chicago

Library of Congress Catalog Card Number: 93-78204

ISBN: 0-942641-47-7

This publication is designed to provide accurate and authoritative information in regard to the subject matter covered. However, it is sold with the understanding that the publisher and author are not engaged in rendering legal or professional investment services. If legal advice or other expert assistance is required, a competent professional should be retained.

Table
of Contents

Preface		**xi**
Introduction		**1**
1	**Market Risk, Timing, and Formula Strategies**	**3**
	RISK AND MARKET RETURNS	3
	Market Returns Over Time	3
	Distribution of Market Returns	9
	Risk and Expected Return	13
	MARKET TIMING AND FORMULA STRATEGIES	20
	Timing the Market	20
	Automatic Timing with Formula Strategies	21
	ENDNOTES	23
2	**Dollar Cost Averaging Revisited**	**25**
	DOLLAR COST AVERAGING: AN EXAMPLE	26
	SHORT-TERM PERFORMANCE	28
	Over One-Year Periods	30
	Over Five-Year Periods	32
	LONG-TERM PROBLEMS WITH DOLLAR COST AVERAGING	34
	Growth Equalization	35
	SUMMARY	36
	ENDNOTES	37
3	**Value Averaging**	**39**
	VALUE AVERAGING: AN INTRODUCTION	39
	SHORT-TERM PERFORMANCE	43

LONG-TERM PERFORMANCE AND VALUE
    AVERAGING   47
    Linear, or Fixed-Dollar, Strategies   47
    Adjusting Strategies for Growth   51
SUMMARY   53
ENDNOTES   54

4   Investment Goals with Dollar Cost Averaging   57

BACKGROUND   57
    Lump-Sum Investments   57
    Using the Formula   59
    Annuities: Periodic Investments   60
    Dollar Cost Averaging and Annuities   63
READJUSTING THE INVESTMENT PLAN   63
    The Readjustment Process   64
    Flexibility   66
    Down-Shifting Investment Risk   69
GROWTH-ADJUSTED DOLLAR COST AVERAGING   71
    Exact Formula   72
    Approximate Formula   74
    Readjusting the DCA Plan   75
SUMMARY   80
ENDNOTES   80
    Appendix to Chapter 4: Constructing a DCA
        Readjustment Spreadsheet   83

5   Establishing the Value Path   87

VALUE AVERAGING VALUE PATHS   87
    The Value Path Formula   88
    Flexible Variations on the Value Path Formula   89
    Readjusting the VA Plan   92
    A Cautionary Note   93
    An Alternate Method   93
SUMMARY   94
ENDNOTES   95
    Appendix to Chapter 5: Constructing a VA
        Readjustment Spreadsheet   97

6 Avoiding Taxes and Transaction Costs   101

TAX CONSIDERATIONS WITH VALUE AVERAGING 101
   The Advantage of Deferred Gains   101
   Deferring Capital Gains Taxes: An Example 102
   A Compromise: No-Sell Value Averaging   107
REDUCING TRANSACTION COSTS   111
   Limiting Taxes   111
   Limiting Costs   112
SUMMARY   113
ENDNOTES   114

7 Playing Simulation Games   117

WHY SIMULATIONS?   117
WHAT AND HOW?   118
   Parameters   118
   Expected Return   119
   Expected Variability   120
   Randomness   120
CONSTRUCTING THE SIMULATION   121
   An Example   122
ENDNOTES   126
   Appendix to Chapter 7: Constructing a Simulation 129
      ENDNOTES TO APPENDIX TO CHAPTER 7   133

8 Comparing the Strategies   135

FIVE-YEAR SIMULATION RESULTS   135
   Using Growth Adjustments   139
   No-Sell Variation   142
   Volatility   143
TWENTY-YEAR SIMULATION RESULTS   145
SUMMARY   146
ENDNOTES   147

9 Profiting from Overreaction   **149**

TIRING OF A RANDOM WALK   149
  Mean Reversion and Overreaction   150
  A Brief Look at the Data   151
WHY DOES THIS MATTER?   160
  Timing   161
ENDNOTES   164

10 Details: Getting Started   **169**

USING MUTUAL FUNDS   169
  The Fund versus Stock Choice   169
  Index Funds   171
  Information on Specific Funds   172
WORKING OUT THE DETAILS   175
  Using a Side Fund   176
  Operating Within a Retirement Account   177
  Establishing a Value Path   178
  Setting Up a VA Value Path: An Example   181
  Other Important Considerations   184
  Using Guidelines and Limits   185
NOTES FOR FINANCIAL PLANNERS   186
  Advanced Methods   187
SUMMARY   189
ENDNOTES   189

11 Examples: Strategies at Work   **193**

THE GOAL AND INVESTMENT ENVIRONMENT   194
  Choosing an Investment   194
  Setting the Goal (Dealing with Inflation)   197
  How Much Should He Invest?   199
INVESTMENT RETURN AND TAKES   200
  Expected Return   200
  Taxes   200

IMPLEMENTING DOLLAR COST AVERAGING 202
  1981: Setting Up DCA 203
  1982-1983 Investment Results 205
  1983: Reassessment and Readjustment 205
  The 1985 Readjustment 211
  And So On and So On . . . 212
  Wrapping It Up: 1991 Results 214
IMPLEMENTING VALUE AVERAGING 215
  Establishing the Value Path 215
  1983: Readjusting the VA Plan 217
  Future VA Readjustments 219
  VA Investments 220
SUMMARY 225
KEY FORMULAS 226
ENDNOTES 227

12 A Final Word **229**

Index **231**

Preface

This book evolved out of an article I wrote titled "Value Averaging: A New Approach to Accumulation," published in the *AAII Journal* X, no. 7 (August 1988). That article introduced an effective formula investment strategy that was a bit more complex than dollar cost averaging (constant dollar investing) but provided higher returns and other potential advantages. Over time, over a thousand investors called or wrote me with several questions, comments, enhancements, or other ideas. So this book was written with investors in mind—investors who want a clean and easy system for accumulating and moving their wealth through time to achieve their financial goals. It's not for investors who want to get rich quick; getting rich *slow* is a noble enough financial goal to achieve.

After trying the latest gimmicks and following the current gurus in a futile quest to outwit and beat the market, some investors are actually satisfied with a fair return for the risk taken with their investment dollar. And, as you'll see in Chapter 1, the stock market really *does* provide a good return over time; there just doesn't seem to be much guidance for the intelligent individual investor on how to achieve these reasonable investment goals effectively. In this book, I attempt to provide and analyze some reasonable and effective ways to build up wealth over time. As opposed to haphazardly jumping from one fad to another, I recommend some disciplined, systematic approaches that allow you to build wealth in a consistent manner and generate good returns without undue risk. Using a systematic approach that is mechanical and nearly automatic relieves the investor of any need for market-timing skills, stock-picking skills, and the emotional involvement in the market that so often turns would-be investors into speculators.

If this all sounds a bit boring, then so be it. Perhaps you will miss the excitement and peril of second-guessing every trade and timing decision you make. Or you might become bored with deciding what to do with the hundreds of dollars you save on newsletters and stock guides, or how to spend all the hours you'll free up.

The book is designed to first give you an overview of the market and a few basic formula strategies for investing in it. Chapter 1 delves into stock market risk and return, so that you are familiar with the investment terrain. Chapters 2 and 3 (respectively) summarize *dollar cost averaging* and *value averaging*, two basic formula strategies. The remainder of the book is oriented toward helping you decide on and tailor an investment strategy that meets *your* needs, so that you can easily map out and immediately start your investment plan. Chapters 4 and 5 provide the methods and give examples of how to set and adjust the amount you invest over time to achieve your investment goals. There are some new formulas and procedures in these chapters that will allow you to respond to inflation, market growth, and many of the uncertainties you will face as your goals and investment performance change over time. Chapter 6 analyzes several important enhancements to these formula strategies and discusses how to deal with taxes and other transaction costs.

Up to this point, all of the data analysis is based on more than six decades of actual historical market data. Chapter 7 introduces you to *market simulations*, used to "game" how a strategy might perform in a wide range of potential future markets. Chapter 8 uses both market simulations and historical data to compare the performance of the two formula strategies and their many variations. Chapter 9 focuses on the tendency for market price movements to overreact. This tendency provides an additional rationale for formula investing; it also highlights the role of formula strategies in taking advantage of excessive price movements, instead of letting them take advantage of you. Chapter 10 provides some usable guidelines and nitty-gritty details for investors and financial planners on how to best use the strategies to meet their individual needs. Chapter 11 follows an investor through a 10-year case study of investing with these two strategies. Real world problems like dealing with inflation, taxes, market surprises, and changing rates of return are examined in detail. Chapter 12 summarizes.

Value Averaging: The Safe and Easy Strategy for Higher Investment Returns provides enough complexity for those readers who really want to "dig into" the material; but most of the tough parts can be skimmed or skipped by casual readers without affecting their ability to construct a reasonable, workable investment strategy. A calculator (especially an inexpensive financial calculator) will come in handy in working through some of the material. And although a computer isn't necessary, readers who have facility with spreadsheet software (e.g., Lotus 1-2-3, Quattro Pro, Excel, etc.) will probably want to experiment on their own with a few of the ideas and perhaps even customize their own plan on their computer. Appendixes following Chapters 4, 5, and 7 provide specific examples and instructions for using spreadsheets to help with your calculations; these are available on diskette from International Publishing Corporation.

The historical stock market data used in many of the analyses in this book are market index data from the University of Chicago's Center for Research in Securities Prices (CRSP). The data used are composed of the daily or monthly return (coming from both dividends and price changes) on the combined listed stocks of the NYSE and AMEX markets, all weighted by their total value, or market capitalization. The monthly figures are end-of-month data from December 1925 to December 1991. The daily figures are from July 2, 1962, to December 31, 1991.

I would like to acknowledge the valued contributions of: Bruce Cohen, Barbara Craig, Jerry Edgerton, Carole Gould, Phil Hamilton, Ronald J. Liszkowski, Alicia Lowe, Vita Nelson, and Maria Scott. My apologies to others whom I should have included. I mention, also, Chris Edleson, because he likes to see his name in print. Special thanks are due to Larry Dillard and Manny Contreras, who provided valuable research assistance. Finally, I dedicate this book to Jan, who, for all of her support, has still not read the book.

Introduction

"Buy low, sell high!" Or so we've been told. Lots of investors have this incredible knack (which they invariably deny) for "buying high" and "selling low." It's easy to get trapped into following the psychology of the market, what with all the excitement generated by the media and the market itself. It takes a lot of guts to buy into the stock market when it's at the very bottom—first of all because you never know when you've arrived at its bottom and second because just about everything you read at the end of a bear market is full of despair and doom. On the other hand, most investors have found out through painful experience that the easiest (and worst!) time to buy stocks is when everyone is euphorically proclaiming the immortality of a soon-to-be-ended bull market.

Market timers and fundamental analysts have their own methods of trying to make this investment dictum come true. Even so, the rest of us who are too busy or too realistic to try calling turns in the market have not been totally left out in the cold. Although we *can* join in their "beat the market" games, we are far less experienced, informed, and capitalized than they are. We can buy their assistance, but often at a price that may exceed its actual value, if any. Or we can strike out on our own, despite the rough terrain of emotional hills and valleys implied above. Formula strategies are the pack mules that can help you in this journey.

A *formula strategy* is any predetermined plan that will "mechanically" guide your investing. One very naive such formula, for example, is to buy one share of stock every week (not recommended!). The best-known formula plan, discussed in Chapter 2, is *dollar cost averaging*, whereby you *invest the same amount of money in an asset each regular investment period,* regardless of its price.

A flexible variation of this is *value averaging*, a strategy I devised in 1988. The basic formula of value averaging, discussed more fully in Chapter 3, is to *invest whatever is needed to make the value of your asset holdings increase by some preset amount each investment period.*

Other formula strategies call for rebalancing your holdings among asset types; for example, constant-ratio plans dictate that a fixed percentage of your wealth should be held in stocks. Some more active versions of formula strategies are really more like market timing; for example, variable-ratio plans change the proportion in each asset type based on some fundamental or technical indicator (e.g., dividends, P/E ratios, short interest, etc.). *Asset allocation* strategies generally fall into this category. We will focus on the more passive formula strategies—dollar cost and value averaging—which are simpler and less chancey for the investor.

The first three chapters provide some basic information on formula plans, particularly dollar cost averaging and value averaging. The basic notions to grasp are that formula plans help you avoid the herd mentality and its arbitrary and often ill-timed investment shifts; they also help guide you in the general direction of buying lower and possibly selling higher. Dollar cost averaging helps a bit on the "buy low" side, but it provides no guidelines for selling. Value averaging has the effect of exaggerating purchases when the market moves lower, but buying less and sometimes even selling shares when the market moves higher. The latter is a bit more complex but well worth considering, given the added flexibility and generally higher returns. All of these issues will be analyzed at length in the chapters to follow.

Market Risk, Timing, and Formula Strategies 1

Whether you call it *investing* or *playing the market*, buying and selling stocks is risky business—risky but lucrative. In choosing to read this book, you have likely decided to build an investment portfolio that may include some of those risky stocks in order to garner some of those lucrative rewards. Before making investment decisions, you should have a reasonable idea of the typical risks you will face in the stock market and the likely rewards you might expect to earn. This chapter provides an introduction to these issues and familiarizes you with some historical data on market performance.

RISK AND MARKET RETURNS

First we will look at the investment returns that have been earned in the stock market in the past. Later in this section we discuss the risk inherent in these returns. Together, this information will provide you with a realistic sense of your opportunities in the stock market.

Market Returns over Time

When any wise market prognosticator is asked the inevitable question: *Is the stock market going to move up or down?*, the unsatisfying but correct answer is: *Yes, it will.* Day-to-day movements are anyone's guess, but over time the market has risen substantially. Stock price movements for the past 66 years are shown in Figure 1-1.[1]

Figure 1-1 MONTHLY STOCK PRICE LEVELS, 1926–1991

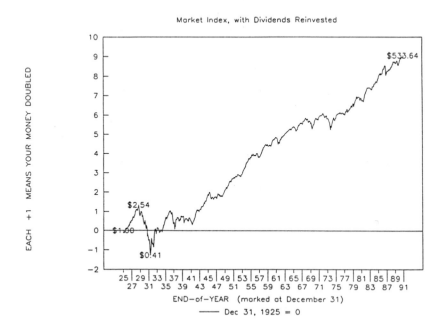

Market Index, with Dividends Reinvested

EACH +1 MEANS YOUR MONEY DOUBLED

END–of–YEAR (marked at December 31)

—— Dec 31, 1925 = 0

The average value of all listed NYSE and AMEX stocks, with all dividends reinvested. A doubling scale is used. Moving from 0 to 1 or from 6 to 7 means the value doubled. A move from 0 to -1 means the value halved.

Note that a $1.00 investment on the last day of 1925 would have been worth $533.64 by the end of 1991. That's a 9.98% compounded annual return over a period where inflation averaged 3.2%. Of course, you could have invested $2.54 prior to the October 1929 stock market crash and despaired as it went as low as $0.41 by mid-1932, losing over five-sixths of its value. Even though there has been only one such period in the past century, this scenario still highlights the magnitude of the potential risks faced when investing in the stock market.

Figure 1-2 MONTHLY STOCK RETURNS, 1926–1991

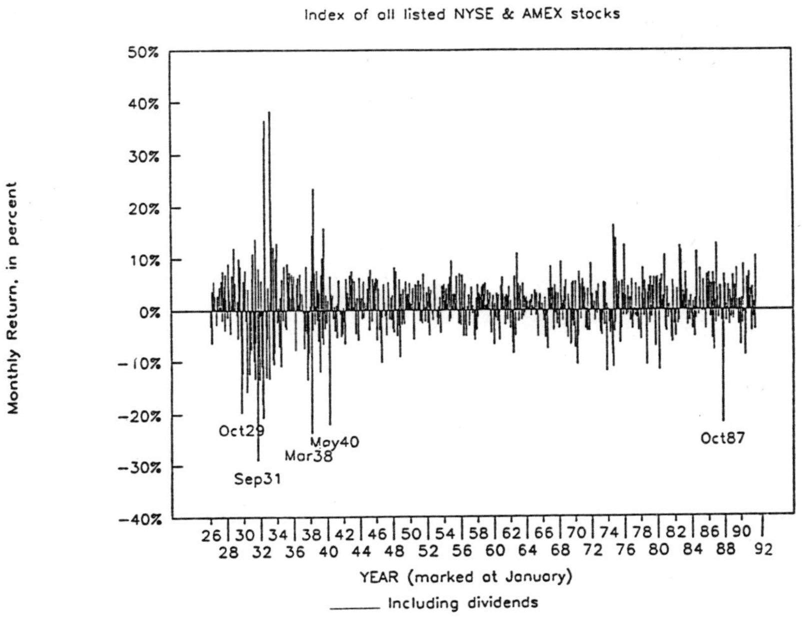

Index of all listed NYSE & AMEX stocks

Each bar on this chart shows the monthly total return on the stock market for each month between January 1926 and December 1991. These returns are *not* annualized.

If you (or more likely an ancestor) had invested $100 in the overall market each month during 1926–1991, your investment would have grown to $11,386,000, more than 140 times the total number of dollars you would have invested. Now admittedly, $100 a month was a lot of money back in the 1930s (worth about $800 in today's dollars), but so is $11 million today. Let's take a closer look at the type of risk entailed in attaining these investment rewards.

Figure 1-2 shows the total return (capital gains *plus* dividends) for each individual month in the 66-year period. Although it is extremely unusual for the market to move more than 20% in a given month, you can see that it *has* happened about ten times. The average market return for one month is slightly under +1.0% (0.95% monthly), or 12% annualized.[2] (See "Returns and Compounding" in the box on page 7.)

Figure 1-3 portrays similar data, but for years instead of months. Here it is easier to see that the market generally goes up, but that there is still random variability with no apparent pattern. The range of returns is from a -44% loss to a +58% gain, although since World War II they fall in a tighter range of -28% to +51%. Individual stocks, of course, exhibit much more variability than the market as a whole, so avoid confusing *typical* market returns with what might happen to a *single* stock.

Figure 1-3 ANNUAL STOCK RETURNS, 1926–1991

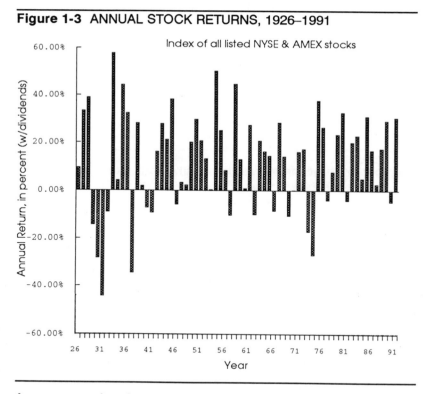

Average annual total return for the stock market, 1926–1991 = +12.0%.

RETURNS and COMPOUNDING

A *return* on investment (e.g., 8%) must be connected with a period of time (e.g., a year). Annual terms are commonly used, but not always. When we shift our concern from one time period to a different one, we must "translate" the return figure as well.

Suppose the total return on a 2-year investment was 21%. A natural way of stating this would be to convert the 2-year return into an annual figure—a 1-year return. But simply dividing the 21% by 2, yielding an annual return figure of 10.50%, would be incorrect. Simple "averaging" of a return ignores *compounding*. Suppose you had a $100 two-year investment, and made a 10.50% return on it in the first year. That gives you $110.50. With another 10.50% return in the second year, you end up with $122.10 (10.50% of $110.50 is $11.60). This is a 2-year return of 22.10%, not just 21%. Actually, a 21% two-year return is equivalent to a 10% annual return ($100 + 10% = $110; $110 + 10% = $121, a 21% total return).

If a is the annual return, then this formula will give you the compound return for n-years:

$$(1 + a)^n = 1 + n\text{-year return}$$

In the example above, $a = 10\%$ and $n = 2$, so:

$$(1 + 0.10)^2 = 1.21 = 1 + n\text{-year return}$$
$$0.21 = 21\% = 2\text{-year return}$$

The process works in reverse, too, to find the annual return given a longer-period return. Taking the n-th root (on a calculator, that's raising something to the $1/n$ power), the formula is:

$$1 + a = {}^{n\text{-th root}}(1 + n\text{-year return})$$
or, $$1 + a = (1 + n\text{-year return})^{1/n}$$

EXAMPLE: What annual rate gets you a 50% return over five years?

$$1 + a = {}^{5\text{-th root}}(1 + 0.50) = (1.50)^2 = 1.0845$$
$$a = 8.45\% \text{ annual return}$$

This process can also be used for calculating compound returns for periods that are *less* than a year in length. Using the top formula, what is the monthly compound return if you get a 12% annual return? HINT: One month is 1/12 of one year.

$$(1 + 0.12)^{1/12} = 1.0095 = 1 + monthly \; return$$
$$0.0095 = 0.95\% = monthly \; return$$

A more general way to write the formula is helpful in translating monthly rates into annual. Suppose that your *long* time period is n times as long as your *short* time period. Then the per period compound returns are related as follows:

$$(1 + short \; period \; return)^n = 1 + long \; period \; return$$

Suppose you could earn 1.0% each month on an investment. What is the annual return? Here, the short period return is 0.01, and $n = 12$:

$$(1.01)^{12} = 1.1268 = 1 + long \; (annual) \; return$$
$$0.1268 = 12.68\% = annual \; return$$

This is the proper method of converting between monthly and annual return figures, and it is used throughout this book.

Even though the market is indeed risky, there is some truth to the statement *Time heals all wounds.* This is evident in Figure 1-4a, where instead of looking at one-year investments we look at four-year periods. Only the worst period (the Great Depression) shows a loss. The annualized return over longer time periods is less variable, because the randomness of the returns causes them to "average out."

Figure 1-4a ANNUALIZED STOCK RETURNS, 1926–1989

Average Annual Return over 4-Year Periods

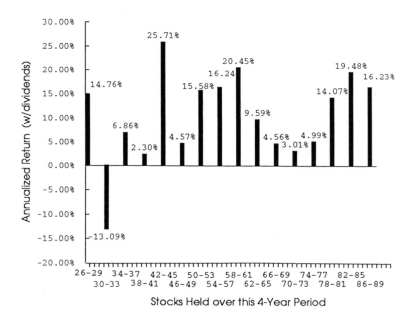

The 64 years from 1926–1989 are divided into 16 4-year investment periods; 1990 and 1991 are omitted. The total return on the stock market over each 4-year period is then annualized.

We could also look at the most recent 64 years, sliced into 4-year periods beginning in 1928. This similar analysis is shown in Figure 1-4b; the results differ slightly. While still less

Figure 1-4b ANNUALIZED STOCK RETURNS, 1928-1991

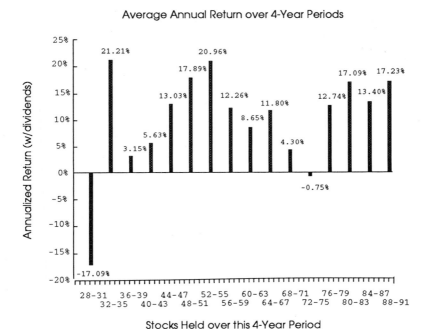

Average Annual Return over 4-Year Periods

variable than single-year returns, these 4-year returns show a different pattern with more losses.

Distribution of Market Returns

The risky nature of the stock market causes many people to mistakenly view it as a form of gambling. Yes, the outcome is uncertain and, as in a casino, you can lose your money. But in the stock market the "house" doesn't take a cut (although your broker or management company certainly will). *On average,* you will lose money in a casino; on average, you will win money or earn some positive return in the stock market (e.g., the +12% average noted above). In either case, the longer you "play" the more certain these outcomes are. Also, unlike the potentially disappearing bankroll you take into the casino, there is no way the value of your *diversified* stock portfolio or fund will ever go to zero (even though any *individual* stock might).

Let's have a look at the historical data on market gains and losses—it is quite interesting and instructive. There were 792 months of market return data between 1926 and 1991; also, daily data were analyzed from the period July 1962 to December 1991. The results are tabulated in Table 1-1. Almost 55% of the daily returns were positive—in a typical 22-day month the market would have had 12 up days and 10 down days. For longer periods, note the increasing probability of a gain in the market over that period.

The market tends to rise over time. Over just a brief instant of "market time," this trend is indiscernible. Over a full day, you can see the tendency; but the random "bounce" around the trend still causes a large number (45½%) of down periods. But as we allow more time, the upward trend compounds, while at the same time the random bounces average each other out.   So as time increases, we are more assured of

TABLE 1-1 Counting the Stock Market's Ups and Downs					
Investment Period	**Total #**	**# Up**		**# Down**	
Days (July 62 - 91)	7,419	4,036	55½%	3,383	45½%
Five-day Periods	1,484	852	57%	632	43%
Months	792	490	62%	302	38%
Years	66	49	74%	17	26%
Four-Year Periods*	16	14½	91%	1½	9%

*Average of 1926-1989 and 1928-1991

getting a positive return out of the market. This characteristic of the market explains the typical advice from investment advisors to put into the stock market only your "five-year-and-out" funds. That is, if you might need access to your funds within the next five years or sooner, it may not all still be there (if invested in the stock market) due to risk of loss; but funds invested for longer periods are less likely to experience a loss.

We can also look at the actual distribution of returns over various time periods to develop a better sense of the risk of the marketplace. A histogram, or bar chart, of annual returns is shown in Figure 1-5, which has a different format from the

Figure 1-5 DISTRIBUTION OF 1-YEAR STOCK RETURNS

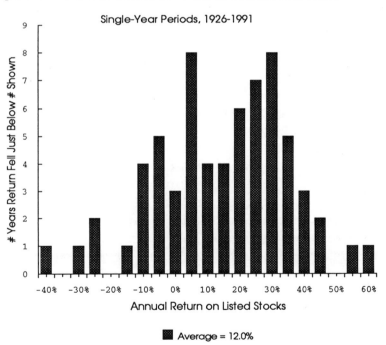

Single-Year Periods, 1926-1991

Average = 12.0%

Histograms showing the distribution of annual stock returns. Example: the bar at -10% shows that on 4 occassions, the annual return fell in the range between -15% and -10%.

previous ones; now the annual return is shown along the horizontal axis. The *number of times* that a particular return occurs is on the vertical axis. The annual returns are grouped into ranges of five percentage points. Reading from left to right, we see that there was one year during which the return was below -40%, one year when it was between -35% and -30%, and two years when it fell by -30% to -25%. You can verify this by looking again at the time series of annual returns in Figure 1-3 above. Note that even though the distribution is centered over the 12% average annual return, the actual return has fallen in the +10% to +15% range during only four years out of the 66 years in the sample. Thus, if one were to say "The expected return on the market is 12%," this would not mean that we really *expect* the return to be +12%. Instead, this statement of *expectation* really means that *on average,* we expect the random returns to vary around (or to center on) +12%. After the fact, of course, we can disparage any such predictions; but this does not mean there is no need for (or value in) making reasoned predictions at all. Pro football quarterbacks manage to keep their jobs despite the self-proclaimed superiority of thousands of Monday-morning quarterbacks.

Figure 1-6 takes the stock returns from four-year periods (also shown year by year in Figure 1-4b) and similarly displays the distribution of returns. Whereas the center (12%) of the distribution doesn't change, the variability decreases. There are no prolonged huge gains or losses, as there were over the shorter single-year periods. Figure 1-7 breaks the last 64 years into eight 8-year periods and displays the distribution of returns. Over this very long time period, the variability of returns was quite small, ranging from no gain to a 16.5% (annual average) gain. Over very long periods, we see neither serious losses nor extreme gains in the stock market.

Figure 1-6 DISTRIBUTION OF 4-YEAR STOCK RETURNS

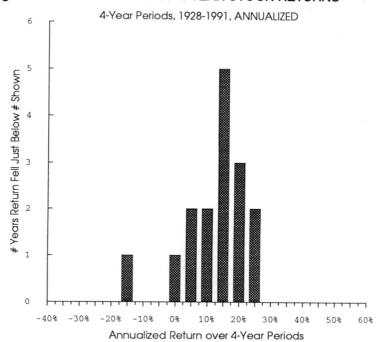

4-Year Periods, 1928-1991, ANNUALIZED

Histograms showing the distribution of annualized returns on the stock market over 4-year periods.

Risk and Expected Return

Different types of investments will be "rewarded" with different expected returns. Both common sense and the historical data tell us this. We now examine the historical performance of a few basic types of investments and apply these lessons of the past to estimate what you can expect from your investments (on average) in the future.

Investments of increasing risk[3] have historically provided higher returns. Figure 1-8 shows the average annual return over

Figure 1-7 DISTRIBUTION OF 8-YEAR STOCK RETURNS

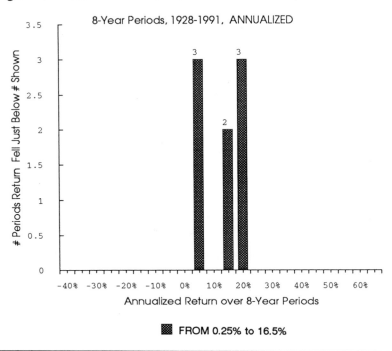

Histogram showing the distribution of annualized returns on the stock market over 8-year periods.

the 1926–1991 period for four broad classes of assets[4], and it displays them in relationship to the average 3.2% inflation rate for the period.

The shortest term Treasury bills bear almost no price risk (variability), but have returned only 3.8% on average; that's only about one-half percent over inflation. Longer-term Treasury bonds returned 5.1%, over a percentage point higher for taking the extra price risk. Bond prices can exhibit a lot of variation, as bond investors were surprised to find out over the past two decades. Corporate bonds are even riskier because they experience the same "duration-based" price risk that long-term Treasuries do, plus additional risk associated with default.

Figure 1-8 AVERAGE INVESTMENT RETURNS, 1926-1991

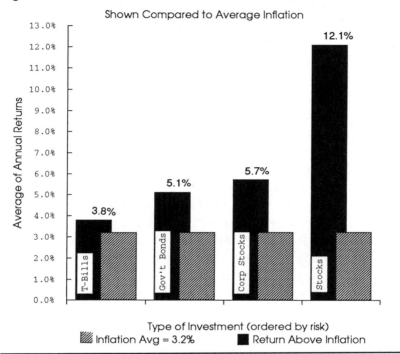

Average annual returns on various financial instruments, 1926–1991. Stocks earned 8.9% over the 3.2% average inflation rate, and 7.0% more than the return on government bonds.

The reward for these risks over time has not been great; top-grade corporates returned 5.7% over the period, or about one-half point more than Treasuries. The stock market has garnered far higher returns, which should not be surprising now that you are familiar with the high level of risk that had to be borne in the market. The 12.1% average return on stocks exceeds inflation by 8.9%, beats out T-bills by 8.3%, and surpasses the return on government bonds by 7.0%.

What about the future? Do the 66 years of returns analyzed portend a 12% expected annual return for the future?

Not quite. First, there is no guarantee that the next 66 years will be anything like the past. Second, it is the *relative* return, not the *absolute* return, that gives us potentially useful information from past results. That is, if the basic risk differences between stocks and bonds persist into the future, then the basic return differences between them will probably continue as well. Higher returns will be demanded by investors to take the higher risk inherent in stocks, so, on average, stocks will have to give higher returns than bonds. The most relevant number to project into the future seems to be the 7% difference between common stock and government bond returns. With long-term government bond rates at 7–8% as of 1992, this would make the expected return on the stock market *14–15%*. Although the assumptions that go into this projected return are reasonable, different sets of assumptions could result in very reasonable market return projections in the 12% to 16% range.

Now we can factor in the expected *risk* with this expected *return* to get a rough assessment of the probability of likely outcomes if you are invested in the stock market. Annual returns in the market had a standard deviation of 20.8% over the period analyzed. (See "Risk and Standard Deviation" in the box on page 17.)

For a normal distribution, about two-thirds of repeated outcomes will fall into a range within one standard deviation of the average. That is, about two-thirds of the area under the relative likelihood curve would occur between -1 and +1 for the standard normal distribution as shown in Figure 1-9.

For stock returns, about two-thirds of the years' returns should fall into a range within one standard deviation of the average; for the past, this is roughly between -9% and +33%, using 12% as the center. Likewise, about 95% of the returns should fall into a range within two standard deviations on either side of the average.

So what's likely to happen in future years in the stock-market? Using the reasonable *expectations* of a 15% return and a 20% standard deviation around that expected return, we can

RISK and STANDARD DEVIATION

Whenever an outcome (such as next year's return on the stock market) is random, it could take on many likely values. These outcomes or possible values have some expected value—also called the mean or average or center—around which they might "fall." Suppose this average is 15%; that means that the possible outcomes, while random, will center on 15%. It would be nice to know *how closely* the possible returns occur near the average. If the *spread* of possible random returns is very large—say, if -50% and +60% returns were very likely—then we would say that the *distribution* of the random returns around their expected value (average) is very *risky*. The *risk* is that the actual outcome could end up very far (in either direction) from the expected value. In a less risky distribution, perhaps values outside the 0% to 30% range would be highly unlikely.

One way to measure this risk is called the *standard deviation*. This measure is, loosely, the typical distance (deviation) of the random value from their expected value (center). To be 1 standard deviation away from the average is not an unusual occurence; to be 2 standard deviations away is unusual; to be 3 standard deviations away is quite rare. More exactly, the standard deviation is the square root of the variance; the variance is the average squared-distance from the expected value. A function (@std) in most spreadsheet packages will calculate the standard deviation of any range for you. The standard deviation is in the same units as the average—percent, in the case of stock returns.

Figure 1-9 is a sketch of the *standard normal distribution* showing the relative likelihood of a random outcome compared to its expected value. Random outcomes are shown along the bottom scale, in terms of how far (how many standard deviations away) they are from the expected value or center. Note that it is most likely that random outcomes are near their expected value, and less and less likely to occur the further they are from their expected value. The probability that an outcome will fall in a particular range is given by the amount of the total area under the "bell-curve" that falls between those two numbers. For example, there is a 38.3% probability that the random value will fall between -0.5 and +0.5 standard deviations from the center. Other probabilities of falling within a certain distance of the expected value are: *68.3% within 1 s.d.; 86.6% within 1.5 s.d.; 95.4% within 2 s.d.; 98.8% within 2.5 s.d.* Only one-quarter of one percent of normal random values would be more than 3 standard deviations from the center.

Thus, a standard deviation is simply a measure of spread that allows us to "standardize" how far random values are spread about their center. This is useful for assessing the likelihood of various stock returns. Figure 1-10 shows one possible random distribution of stock market returns, using the numbers in the text for center (15% expected return) and spread (20% standard deviation). The possible annual returns along the bottom of the sketch are marked in one standard deviation intervals (every 20%, centered around 15%). This allows us to make probability assessments of various returns, as presented in the text.

Figure 1-9 NORMAL DISTRIBUTION

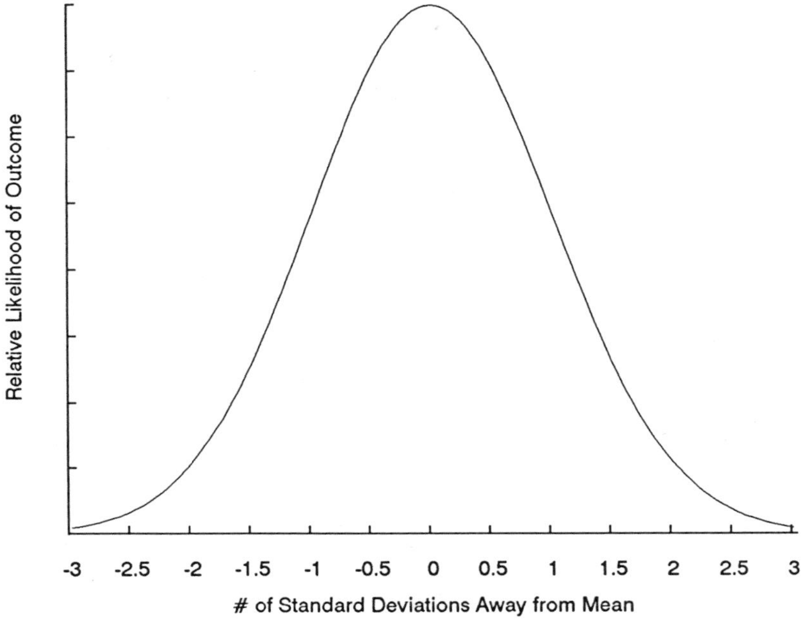

This is a sketch of the "standard normal distribution," as described in the box on page 17 titled "Risk and Standard Deviation." The area under the curve gives the probability of an occurence in a given range.

make these reasoned guesses as to the probability of *future* market outcomes (see Figure 1-10):

● The return should be between -5% and +35% in roughly two out of three years.
● The return should be between -25% and +55% in all but one out of twenty years.
● You will make more than the 6% T-note rate about 67% of the time (two out of three years).

Figure 1-10 POSSIBLE DISTRIBUTION OF STOCK RETURNS

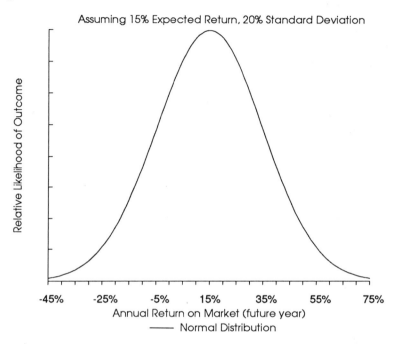

Assuming 15% Expected Return, 20% Standard Deviation

Relative Likelihood of Outcome

-45%   -25%   -5%   15%   35%   55%   75%

Annual Return on Market (future year)
—— Normal Distribution

This shows the relative likelihood of various 1-year stock market return outcomes, assuming the 15% center, 20% spread figures in the text. The area under the curve gives probabilities of ranges.

- You will have a positive return in about 77% of the years and lose money two years out of every nine.
- You will lose more than -10% about one year in ten.
- Your chances of losing money over a full four-year period of investment is only about 6%–7%.
- Over a ten-year period, the odds are 7-to-1 that your market return will average better than the current long-term government bond interest rate.
- The market will have a "big year" of a 25% or higher gain roughly every three years.

These numbers are nothing more than educated guesses backed up by reasonable assumptions and analyses. They are not meant to entice or scare you, only to give you some estimate of what you're getting into. Note that these numbers apply to the returns (including dividends) on the market as a whole, and not to a particular stock, industry, or other undiversified investment. As the advertisements say, "Your mileage may vary!"

MARKET TIMING AND FORMULA STRATEGIES

Being able to time the market is certainly one of every investor's dreams. Knowing when the market has peaked or how to distinguish a *market correction* from the seemingly identical *start of a bear market* is beyond the capabilities of mere mortals (except in retrospect, when many would-be market oracles claim to have accomplished this feat). But our failings are not from lack of trying. There are thousands of market professionals whose main purpose is to "call" turns in the market or to advise investors or clients when to switch between asset types.

Timing the Market

Despite the exhortations of many who study financial markets to assume a buy-and-hold posture in the market, the temptation to actively pursue timing strategies wins over many investors. A look back at the numbers may help you understand why. Using a buy-and-hold strategy, an investor with $100 at the end of 1925 would have accrued $53,364 by the end of 1991 (a 9.98% compound annual return). If this investor had been lucky enough to pull her money out of equity investments just prior to all "down" years and just keep it in a mattress, her 1991 fund would have been $981,848 instead (a 14.94% compound annual return). This would have involved 15 round-trip, end-of-year switches out of and into the stock market. If only 4 well-timed switches had been allowed, instead of 15, she still could have had $526,012 by 1991, a 13.86% compound annual return.

The problem with this is obvious—you just never know beforehand when to move your money into and out of the market. Individual investors, as motivated as they are to buy low and sell high, invariably have this incredible knack for doing just the opposite. It's so easy to get wrapped up in the euphoria of a raging bull market and buy high, or be scared into selling low by the "sky is falling" bear market mentality, that most attempts by small investors to time the market are doomed to failure. Look at a poor investor who had the misfortune to "reverse-time" the market in the worst way over our 66-year market period. By moving into and out of the market at the end of the worst possible years, the $100 in 1925 could have dwindled to roughly the cost of a Big Mac and fries (with no drink) by 1991. I don't personally know any of the extreme investors described above, but we all certainly know of "timers" who more frequently resemble this latter unfortunate case than the former. In fact, many market technicians and professionals tend to use levels of small investor sentiment such as odd-lot sales, mutual fund inflow/outflow statistics, and investor surveys to gauge when the market is overbought or saturated (indicators that are too positive supposedly portend a down market), or when investor depression is a potential precursor to a turn upward.

Automatic Timing with Formula Strategies

The rewards to successful timing are substantial, but individual investors, in particular, seldom reap them. Many investors have found that they need a disciplined approach to help them avoid the herd mentality that often leaves their ill-timed investments underperforming the market. This is where *formula strategies* enter the picture.

Whereas typical timing strategies involve *active* decisions about moving money into and out of the stock market (or other investments), formula strategies are nothing more than *passive* guidelines toward the same end. The idea is to proceed through the twisting, bumpy investment highway on cruise control, avoiding the excessive stop-and-go natural tendencies that seem to brake your investment vehicle in all the wrong places. Formula strategies are meant to be automatic and mechanical, the very antithesis of the emotional involvement inherent in timing strategies. Passive formula investing is *not* meant to beat the market but merely to survive in it and end up with the proper reward for the risk incurred. As we have seen, mere survival in the market grants fairly substantial rewards that grow even more substantial over time. In our greed to beat the market, we often miss that simple point.

Also remember that if timing systems were developed that could truly consistently beat the market, they would not be viable for very long. If we all jumped on the same bandwagon, we'd all get the same return—the *average* return. If you're looking for a surefire way to beat the market, this book will not likely provide it. The formula strategies we'll encounter will provide a few sensible alternative methods of adjusting your market exposure and accumulating market wealth over time. They will, we hope, give you the investment returns you deserve to compensate you for risk while guiding you away from the trap that snares so many investors—that of buying high, then panicking and selling low.

As mentioned earlier, the most popular formula strategy is dollar cost averaging, summarized in Chapter 2. *Value averaging* is a variation of dollar cost averaging that will be introduced in its simplest form in Chapter 3. Several variations of dollar cost averaging and value averaging will be presented and analyzed to help you tailor a strategy that suits your needs. The number of different formula strategies that could be devised is limited only by one's imagination. You will find that no one strategy is strictly better than all the others, but that each has its own specific flavor that will appeal to different investors in different ways. By "paper-trading" many of these strategies against actual market data and simulated possible future markets, as is done in this book, you should be able to get a reasonable feel for the capabilities and limitations of these strategies. This should help you pick out one that is comfortable for you to use in accumulating your own wealth over time.

ENDNOTES

---

1.   All historical market data used are calculated from CRSP daily and monthly value-weighted market index return series. This index takes all stocks listed on the NYSE and AMEX and constructs a weighted average based on each stock's total market capitalization, thus giving an accurate indication of the total value of the combined stocks on both markets.

2.   This 12% average does not contradict the 9.98% compounded growth rate quoted earlier. This higher 12% figure is obtained simply by averaging all of the various annual returns; the lower 9.98% figure is calculated by figuring out the *constant* rate at which the beginning value would have to increase to grow to the final actual value. This is the difference between an *arithmetic* mean and a *geometric* mean. A simple example is a $100 stock that falls to $50 (-50%) one year, and then rebounds (+100%) back to $100 the second year. The arithmetic mean, or average, of the two (-50%, +100%) annual figures is +25%, but the compound annual growth rate to get from beginning ($100) to end ($100) was clearly +0%. Arithmetic means are always higher than geometric means. This means that the *average* of returns from several periods will always be a number higher than the actual *compound return* per period.

3.   The working definition of *risk* as used here is the expected standard deviation (typical variation from the average) of annual returns. This is not exactly the right kind of risk to associate with the expected returns on individual assets—finance practitioners use measures of *market risk* (such as *beta*) for stocks, that are more

complex. But for the purposes used here (differentiating broad classes of assets), the more basic measure of risk works fine.

4.   T-bill and stock data are from CRSP data set. Ibbotson and Sinquefield's *Stocks, Bonds, Bills and Inflation* reports similar numbers for the period ending in 1991. (Chicago: Ibbotson Associates, published annually.) Their numbers are used for bond returns.

Dollar Cost Averaging Revisited 2

Dollar cost averaging (DCA) is a simple and popular formula strategy used by many individual investors as a time-honored way of trying to increase long-run investment returns. As mentioned earlier, the DCA strategy is founded on a simple rule: *invest the same amount of money each time period, regardless of the price.* You accumulate wealth gradually over time through a consistent inflow of investment dollars at a steady rate, during good times and bad.

Sticking to the formula means that you avoid the nervous selling during market panics that leaves so many individual investors on the sidelines later during the inevitable upward turns coming out of a down market. The formula also provides a discipline by which you increase your exposure to market risk and return gradually over time, thus avoiding ill-timed, near-peak investments that entice your dollars into a feeding frenzy at the crest of every bull market wave. Dollar cost averaging is an automatic market timing mechanism that eliminates the need for active market timing. According to John Markese, Ph.D., director of research for the American Association of Individual Investors, "Dollar cost averaging gives you time diversification." This time diversification is different from that seen in Chapter 1. There, we saw that longer investment periods reduced the average annual volatility of the compound annual return—very few long-term investment periods saw a loss. Spreading out your actual purchases over time is a different sort of risk-reducing diversification. When money is invested regularly, the average cost of shares is leveled out over time—over good *and* bad prices. There is little of the risk, associated with lump-sum purchases, of buying into the market with your total investment right at the market peak. If you dollar cost average over *long* periods of time, you can take advantage of *both* forms of time diversification to reduce your investment risk.

The DCA strategy invests a fixed amount at regular intervals (every month for many investors), regardless of market price. Because you end up buying shares at various prices, you get fewer shares when prices are high and more shares when prices are low. This is in line with our natural desire to buy low, and is contrary to most investors' natural reaction to market levels (e.g., to buy high). So then a $100 investment would buy 25 shares at $4 but only 20 shares at a higher price of $5.

DOLLAR COST AVERAGING: AN EXAMPLE

Table 2-1 shows my actual experience in a particular precious metals mutual fund over a two-year period (dividends and distributions have been omitted for simplicity). This fund and the period analyzed are the same as in my original article upon which this book is based. Figures are provided in a later section to update these numbers by including 1988 and 1989 as well. On the 15th of each month, $100 of that fund was purchased; this accumulated over 24 months. The DCA rationale can be seen in the table—more shares were bought when the share price was low, and fewer shares were bought at a high share price. For example, look at the difference between July 1986 and April 1987. Investing $100 at the very low share price of $2.99 purchased more than 33 shares. By the following April, however, investing the same $100 at the inflated $7.47 price bought only 13 shares. Of course, it would have been nicer to *sell* shares that month; but we'll save that thought for Chapter 3.

This loading up on "cheap" shares reduces the average cost of the shares actually purchased by dollar cost averaging to $4.85, which is below the average price of the fund over the 24 months ($5.18). All shares are then valued at the final per-share price of $5.06 in January 1988. A better measure for the success

TABLE 2-1 Example of Dollar Cost Averaging					
Mutual Fund		Dollar Cost Averaging			
Month	Share Price	($$$) Invested	# Shares To Buy	# Shares Owned	Total Value
Jan 86	$4.64	($100)	21.55	21.55	$100
Feb 86	$4.38	($100)	22.83	44.38	$194
Mar 86	$4.56	($100)	21.93	66.31	$302
Apr 86	$4.25	($100)	23.53	89.84	$382
May 86	$3.81	($100)	26.25	116.09	$442
Jun 86	$3.19	($100)	31.35	147.44	$470
Jul 86	$2.99	($100)	33.44	180.88	$541
Aug 86	$3.60	($100)	27.78	208.66	$751
Sep 86	$4.70	($100)	21.28	229.94	$1,081
Oct 86	$4.41	($100)	22.68	252.61	$1,114
Nov 86	$4.34	($100)	23.04	275.65	$1,196
Dec 86	$4.69	($100)	21.32	296.98	$1,393
Jan 87	$5.26	($100)	19.01	315.99	$1,662
Feb 87	$4.54	($100)	22.03	338.01	$1,535
Mar 87	$5.38	($100)	18.59	356.60	$1,919
Apr 87	$7.47	($100)	13.39	369.99	$2,764
May 87	$7.39	($100)	13.53	383.52	$2,834
Jun 87	$6.31	($100)	15.85	399.37	$2,520
Jul 87	$7.07	($100)	14.14	413.51	$2,924
Aug 87	$6.48	($100)	15.43	428.94	$2,780
Sep 87	$7.07	($100)	14.14	443.09	$3,133
Oct 87	$6.96	($100)	14.37	457.46	$3,184
Nov 87	$5.05	($100)	19.80	477.26	$2,410
Dec 87	$5.80	($100)	17.24	494.50	$2,868
Jan 88	$5.06			Final Value:	$2,502
Avg. Price w/CS				Total Cost:	($2,400)
	$5.18			Average Cost Per Share:	$4.85
Internal Rate of Return (IRR):					4.0%

Results of monthly dollar cost averaging over a two-year period, using mid-month prices for an actual precious metals fund. The IRR (not shown) for the constant share purchase "strategy" was -0.2%.

of the dollar cost averaging strategy, because it accounts for the "time-value" of money, is the rate of return, also called *IRR* for *internal rate of return*. See "Internal Rate of Return (IRR)," in the box on page 29. Compounded monthly, and in annual terms, the rate of return is +4% using dollar cost averaging. As a basis for comparison, you could have followed a *constant share purchase* "strategy"; that is, if had you purchased the same number of shares each month, your IRR would have been -0.2%.

The preceding example serves to highlight the two main perceived benefits of dollar cost averaging that have endeared it to investors looking for a way to accumulate shares over time:

- It is simple and easy to apply.
- It increases the rate of return (and reduces the average share cost) of the investment.

Because most mutual funds readily accept automatic monthly transfers of funds from your checking account, dollar cost averaging is a natural choice for investors to use in building their nest eggs.

SHORT-TERM PERFORMANCE

Dollar cost averaging usually does provide higher returns in the stock market over short- and intermediate-term investment periods. The basis of comparison is a constant share (CS) purchase strategy, such as that in Table 2-1.[1] The CS strategy "buys a share of the market" every month at whatever price the "market" (or whatever fund or other investment vehicle you've chosen) is then worth. The average purchase cost of your holdings would simply be the average market price over the investment period. The DCA strategy is then used with monthly frequency over the same market period, and the rates of return (IRR) resulting from the two strategies are compared for each period.

INTERNAL RATE OF RETURN (IRR)

Throughout this book, the terms rate of return, internal rate of return, and IRR are used to describe the investment performance of a particular strategy or of any set of cash flows. A good way to think about this IRR measure is that it is the fixed yield you would have to earn on a bank account that receives all of your investment inflows in order to match the performance of your investment (that is, produce the resulting outflows).

As an example, look at the cash flows for the fund investment in Table 2-1. You put in $100 a month (inflow), getting a wildly random return, finally resulting in a value of $2,502 (outflow). What kind of (fixed) bank rate of return would have produced the same results? Since the investments were at monthly intervals, we must use monthly rates. Try 0.5% first (6.17% annually): If you'd invested $100 each month at this monthly rate, you would have accrued $2,556 after 2 years. Your investment only achieved $2,502, though, so your IRR must have been below 0.5% monthly. Trying 0.3%, the result would be $2,492—you did better than this, so your IRR is above 0.3% monthly. It turns out that 0.33% monthly would have accumulated about $2,502, so we say that the internal rate of return (IRR) is 0.33% monthly, which is 4.03% annually. We generally convert the IRR so that we consistently quote it in annual terms (see box on converting rates in Chapter 1 on page 7).

Remember that the IRR is simply that rate of return that would have provided the same cash flows or investment results as the investment that you're analyzing. Thus, it can apply in situations with different cash flows that are more complex than the DCA example just examined. Suppose in 1987 (assume all cash flows occur at the beginning of each year) you invested $1,000 and received a $60 dividend a year later. Then in 1989 you received another $60 dividend, but invested another $500. You then sell most of your shares for $900 in 1990, and the remainder of your shares are valued at $802 a year later in 1991. Your net cash flows, at 1-year intervals, are:

1987	-$1,000
1988	+ 60
1989	- 440
1990	+ 900
1991	+ 802

By trial and error you can calculate the IRR to be 7.5% annually. That is, if the cash flows had all earned 7.5% each year, all the inflows and outflows would be accounted for. Suppose you had $1,000 in a bank at 7.5%—could you replicate these cash flows exactly? $1,000 at 7.5% gives you $1,075 by 1988, or $1,015 after taking out $60. That $1,015 grows to $1,091 by 1989; then adding $440 makes balance $1,531, which grows at 7.5% interest to $1,646 in 1990. Taking out $900 leaves you with $746, which grows to $802 by 1991. Take out $802 and the "account" has provided all of the required cash flows. Thus 7.5% was the correct figure for the internal rate of return.

Luckily, you don't have to do any of this trial and error calculation. Computer spreadsheets have an "@IRR" function that does it for you; see your software manual.

Over One-Year Periods

In Table 2-2, the rates of return from using the two strategies are compared for each year of actual stock market history (1926–1991). With dollar cost averaging, $100 is invested at the beginning of each month,[2] and the portfolio is valued on the last day of the year, after 12 equal monthly investments.

Of the 66 annual periods analyzed, dollar cost averaging had a higher return 51 times, tied twice, and was beaten by the constant share strategy on 13 occasions. When DCA "won," it provided relative returns as much as 9.97 percentage points higher than CS (in 1933) and averaged 0.71% higher when it won. When DCA "lost," its relative returns were never more than -0.57 percentage points lower than CS (in 1954); the average DCA return was only 0.24% lower than CS on those few occasions that it lost.

The monthly figures for 1954 are provided here to give an example of when DCA fares poorly. The average cost per "share" of the market was $900.03 with CS and only $891.14 with DCA. DCA will *always* have a lower share price; but the DCA return can be lower in a particularly good or bad year, such as 1954. In this year, CS would have purchased more shares during the early months because the price rise reduced DCA share purchases. Due to the rapid acceleration in the last two months, these extra CS-purchased shares (even though a bit more expensive) really paid off.

Monthly Market Level Figures for 1954

Beginning of	Market Level	Beginning of	Market Level
January	752.73	July	909.66
February	790.80	August	955.53
March	805.98	September	934.00
April	836.43	October	994.06
May	872.08	November	977.92
June	899.43	December	1071.76
		End of Year	**1131.01**

TABLE 2-2 Comparison of (monthly) DCA vs. CS Rates of Return Over 1-Year Periods: 1926–1991					
Year	CS	DCA	Year	CS	DCA
26	17.86%	18.07%	60	11.87%	12.03%
27	36.41%	36.41%	61	20.79%	20.95%
28	*48.63%*	*48.37%*	62	2.99%	4.63%
29	-33.55%	-32.31%	63	17.35%	17.48%
30	*-45.39%*	*-45.46%*	64	12.93%	13.04%
31	*-59.76%*	*-60.22%*	65	15.48%	15.52%
32	3.73%	11.25%	66	- 6.17%	- 5.74%
33	41.33%	51.30%	67	19.23%	19.55%
34	2.35%	3.11%	68	19.27%	19.62%
35	*66.72%*	*66.43%*	69	- 9.90%	- 9.71%
36	34.22%	34.34%	70	20.87%	22.45%
37	*-47.38%*	*-47.67%*	71	12.89%	13.09%
38	41.10%	43.06%	72	*17.15%*	*17.11%*
39	15.96%	16.72%	73	-15.82%	-15.64%
40	-0.31%	0.77%	74	-27.74%	-26.84%
41	-12.23%	-11.89%	75	14.35%	15.74%
42	33.37%	33.65%	76	18.32%	18.44%
43	11.17%	12.08%	77	1.34%	1.45%
44	22.49%	22.49%	78	6.74%	7.46%
45	*41.87%*	*41.75%*	79	21.49%	21.67%
46	-14.02%	-13.22%	80	38.74%	39.30%
47	7.97%	8.12%	81	- 3.85%	- 3.63%
48	-1.30%	- 0.73%	82	44.37%	44.85%
49	*33.21%*	*33.07%*	83	11.80%	12.45%
50	*35.89%*	*35.61%*	84	12.81%	13.03%
51	18.63%	18.73%	85	*30.87%*	*30.73%*
52	*18.17%*	*18.13%*	86	6.23%	6.83%
53	6.13%	6.30%	87	-22.92%	-21.14%
54	*53.71%*	*53.14%*	88	12.63%	12.74%
55	25.61%	25.71%	89	22.15%	22.71%
56	6.18%	6.41%	90	-0.38%	0.12%
57	-16.90%	-16.65%	91	25.99%	26.07%
58	50.12%	49.72%	Avg IRR	12.02%	12.61%
59	11.84%	11.93%			

Investment frequency is monthly. Rate of return is annualized IRR. *Italicized* entries are for years in which CS strategy outperformed DCA.

Note that during recent decades, DCA has done quite well. Throughout all 66 years, dollar cost averaging returned an average 12.61%, or 0.59% higher than the share-a-month (CS) return of 12.02%. The relative potential "danger" of the DCA strategy is quite minimal, but sometimes the rewards are substantial.[3] One further point, related to the data in Chapter 1, concerns the frequency of loss. Of 66 years, there were 17 years in which stock prices were down; but only 14 of the annual returns from using dollar cost averaging were negative. This highlights the risk reduction due to time diversification.

Over Five-Year Periods

In Table 2-3, the rates of return from using the two strategies is compared for all possible (overlapping) 5-year periods of actual stock market history (1926–1930 through 1987–1991). With dollar cost averaging, $100 is invested at the beginning of each month, and the portfolio is valued on the last day of the 5-year period, after 60 equal monthly investments.

Of the 62 five-year periods analyzed, dollar cost averaging had a higher return 52 times and was beaten by the constant share strategy on only 10 occasions (and only 3 times in the past 23 years). When DCA "won," it provided relative annualized returns as much as 7.48 percentage points higher than CS (1929–1933) and averaged 1.02% higher when it won. When DCA "lost," its relative returns were never more than -0.58 percentage points lower than CS (1950–1954); the average DCA return was only 0.24% lower than CS on those few occasions when it lost. Over the entire period, dollar cost averaging returned an average compound annualized return of 0.89% higher than the CS strategy.

The average share price reduction provided by dollar cost averaging gives you a reasonable chance at enhancing your investment rate of return over short- and medium-term investment periods. But as you can see, it plays very little role in your

TABLE 2-3 Comparison of (monthly) DCA vs. CS Rates of Return Over 5-Year Periods: 1926–1930 through 1987–1991							
5 Years From	To	CS	DCA	5 Years From	To	CS	DCA
26	30	-9.90%	-5.64%	58	62	7.04%	7.85%
27	31	-30.63%	-29.24%	59	63	10.28%	10.35%
28	32	-26.63%	-24.16%	60	64	12.71%	12.79%
29	33	-8.42%	-0.94%	61	64	13.42%	13.48%
30	34	-1.14%	4.64%	62	66	5.83%	6.61%
31	35	18.53%	21.73%	63	67	11.98%	12.02%
32	36	30.63%	31.13%	64	68	*12.78%*	*12.69%*
33	37	-0.41%	4.15%	65	69	4.09%	4.58%
34	38	6.87%	8.76%	66	70	2.84%	3.34%
35	39	4.30%	5.77%	67	71	6.40%	6.68%
36	40	-1.03%	-0.30%	68	72	10.22%	10.45%
37	41	-4.03%	-3.43%	69	73	0.68%	1.33%
38	42	3.99%	4.35%	70	74	-11.39%	-10.34%
39	43	11.06%	11.43%	71	75	0.19%	0.82%
40	44	16.33%	16.55%	72	76	7.97%	8.81%
41	45	*25.97%*	*25.56%*	73	77	5.82%	6.54%
42	46	14.72%	16.63%	74	78	7.98%	8.55%
43	47	8.73%	9.94%	75	79	12.76%	12.79%
44	48	4.89%	5.80%	76	80	*19.44%*	*19.01%*
45	49	8.92%	9.07%	77	81	12.22%	12.75%
46	50	*16.03%*	*16.00%*	78	82	15.82%	15.97%
47	51	*20.41%*	*20.19%*	79	83	17.81%	17.95%
48	52	19.52%	19.76%	80	84	13.52%	13.95%
49	53	12.87%	13.99%	81	85	*19.48%*	*19.43%*
50	54	*23.35%*	*22.77%*	82	86	19.25%	19.78%
51	55	*24.64%*	*24.15%*	83	87	10.68%	12.16%
52	56	19.96%	20.58%	84	88	12.09%	13.25%
53	57	7.16%	9.57%	85	89	16.34%	16.62%
54	58	17.18%	17.47%	86	90	7.97%	8.48%
55	59	*15.05%*	*15.03%*	87	91	14.65%	14.63%
56	60	10.72%	11.00%				
57	61	16.53%	16.57%	Avg IRR		9.31%	10.20%

Investment frequency is monthly, for 60 months. Rate of return is annualized IRR. *Italicized* entries are for periods in which CS outperformed DCA strategy.

overall return, compared with the performance of your investment. That is, a bad year is a bad year, even with dollar cost averaging. The investment vehicle you choose (and how it fares) is far more important to your results than the mechanical rules you follow to invest in it. To that end, the best use of dollar cost averaging is for *very diversified* investments, such as a broad-based mutual fund or, preferably, an index fund. These issues will be highlighted in later chapters.

LONG-TERM PROBLEMS WITH DOLLAR COST AVERAGING

Based on the foregoing analysis, you would expect dollar cost averaging to also perform well over longer investment periods. It doesn't. Suppose you had started with a constant share purchase strategy and dollar cost averaging, each with $1 in January 1926,[4] and continued monthly until 1991. (This involves 792 monthly investments, so I'll spare you the table.) The CS strategy (a share a month) would have achieved an annualized rate of return of 11.24% over the period, whereas the DCA strategy ($1 a month) would have yielded only an 11.03% rate of return.

Worse than that, it wouldn't have made much sense to dollar cost average with the same investment amount (be it $1, $100, or any fixed amount) over this entire period. Although the amount contributed each month under CS would have grown over time as the level of the market grew, you always would (with DCA) be investing a single dollar (or some other fixed amount) each month. But, as we are well aware, a 1991 dollar just isn't the same as a 1926 dollar (or even a 1981 dollar for that matter). Due to inflation, today's dollar is only worth one-eighth of its earlier value. So it makes sense, then, to at least take the "fixed amount" invested each month in a DCA plan and adjust it upward for inflation every now and then. Had this been done gradually over the 66 years, the result of using inflation-adjusted[5] dollar cost averaging would have been an annualized rate of return of 11.09%—a little bit higher than before but still under the CS base case of 11.24%. Let's examine why DCA failed.

Even with adjusting for inflation, there is still a problem over the long term because the stock market grows *much* faster than inflation over time. As mentioned previously, $1 of January 1926 market value grew to $533.64 worth of stock market value by 1991. The inflation-adjusted DCA strategy, which starts with a $1 investment buying a "full share" of the market in 1926, is investing only $8, or under 0.02 "shares" of the market by 1991. Our investment in the market is now less than one-fiftieth as large as it was in 1926. Because our investment amount so radically lags behind market growth, our exposure to market risk is not very well balanced over time. In relative terms, we would have poured a lot of money into the 1920–1930 market and very little real investment in the market of the 1980s (a much better market in which to invest). Due to its lack of growth, the dollar cost averaging strategy gradually "fades away" over time, as the new moneys invested become more and more meaningless with respect to how much value they can buy in the fast-growing stock market.

Growth Equalization

The dollar cost averaging strategy doesn't "grow" with the market; this presents both logical and performance problems, as discussed above. The CS strategy, starting with $1 and increasing with the market value, yields a final 1991 portfolio value of $422,106, much more than either version of dollar cost averaging discussed so far.[6] But if the so-called fixed amount of the dollar cost averaging investment had been increased by *some* steady amount over the 66 years, it could have resulted in a 1991 portfolio with roughly this larger value. That is, we could have made the amount invested in a DCA strategy steadily grow enough to keep up with the long-term growth in the level of the market. We can call this a *growth-equalized* variation of the strategy. It works out that, had you increased the original $1 fixed amount each month by 0.64% (a 7.96% annualized growth rate), you would have ended up with a $422,238 portfolio value using this growth-equalized dollar cost averaging strategy, about the same magnitude as the CS portfolio. Your DCA investment would have gradually kept pace with the market—at least enough to compare the results with the CS strategy. The rate of return on DCA would have jumped to 11.46%, higher than the 11.24% rate of return from the CS strategy, and higher still than the two less-sensible versions of dollar cost averaging. Interestingly enough, you wouldn't have needed nearly as much money to invest with growth-equalized dollar cost averaging as with the CS strategy. Whereas the monthly requirement with CS would have bounced up and down (mostly up) with the level of the market to finish at $534/month by 1991, the growing (at 0.64% monthly[7]) DCA requirement would have smoothly increased to $155.44/month by 1991.

The main lesson here is that the investment formula must somehow attempt to keep up with the phenomenal growth in the market over long-term investment periods. This will be even more true with value averaging, as you will see in the next few chapters. Even with a simple strategy like dollar cost averaging, you should increase your investment amount occasionally (every year or two is fine) to keep up with the expected growth in the market. Exactly how to integrate this information into your investment plan will be covered in Chapter 4 (for DCA) and Chapter 5 (for VA).

SUMMARY

Dollar cost averaging is a simple and effective strategy for accumulating investment wealth over time. It knows nothing about whether the market is high or low; it simply works to purchase more shares when the price is lower and fewer shares when it is higher. Therefore, it can't help but reduce the average price of the purchased shares, thus often enhancing the investment rate of return. A good investment vehicle must be utilized, and market growth should be taken into account in determining how much to invest over time.

Dollar cost averaging is a "Buy low, *buy less* high" strategy, as there are no rules for selling. Although we would like to "sell high," no one knows when these highs occur until it is too late. Without guidelines about when to sell, there is always the danger of indiscriminate selling that defeats the motive of accumulation of shares. If that selling takes place during market downturns, as it so frequently does, the results on investment returns can be disastrous.

Even though no rule can tell you accurately when to sell, it turns out that a fairly simple strategy—flexible enough to allow for selling—can significantly improve your long-term results over those attained with dollar cost averaging. Value averaging, introduced in the next chapter, is such a strategy.

ENDNOTES

1. It doesn't make sense to use "buy and hold" as a basis for comparison, which amounts to comparing apples and oranges. As a one-shot purchase, buy and hold does not have the characteristic of *gradually* investing over time. The risk characteristics are totally different. The CS "strategy" is really just a gradual version of buy and hold, because it invests in the same portion (a share) of the market each period and holds it. DCA is just a slight variation on this, so there is some basis for comparing them.

2. Actually, the investment is made at the end of the last day of the prior month. Thus, the first investment for 1933 is made at the December 31, 1932, price. This is the timing for all monthly investments analyzed in this book.

3. This rate or return analysis does not even take into account the apparent benefit of the "time diversification" dollar cost averaging provides. You avoid the risk of entering the market all at once at the

wrong time. Returns are smoothed out over time to the extent that your purchases are smoothed out over time.

4.   The price index for stock market value used in this book is based on a "price" of $1 for the beginning of 1926, growing to over $533 by the end of 1991 (see Figure 1-1).

5.   Monthly averages of short-term T-bill rates are actually used as a proxy for the inflation rate. Over the entire period, they have been quite close, with notable divergences only in the mid-1980s and a few other brief periods.

6.   The $1-a-month fixed DCA strategy results in $113,861 at the end of 1991. Any comparison must keep in mind, though, that the amounts invested in CS and DCA were radically different. By the 1990s, the monthly (1 share) CS investment was over $500, whereas the monthly ($1) DCA investment was still only $1.

7.   In that there was no before-the-fact method of knowing in 1926 that 0.64% was the "right" growth rate, this all might seem a bit artificial. But is is not difficult to estimate a reasonable growth factor based on *expected* market growth. This issue will addressed at length, along with other means of using dollar cost averaging, in Chapter 4.

Value
Averaging 3

This chapter presents a fairly new and simple accumulation strategy, which I call *value averaging,*[1] an alternative approach to investing your money. You may find it useful because it is similar to dollar cost averaging but generally provides a higher rate of return in a long-term investment program.

VALUE AVERAGING: AN INTRODUCTION

Value averaging (VA) is a formula strategy that is more flexible and has a lower average per-share purchase price (and usually a higher rate of return) than dollar cost averaging. Instead of a "fixed dollar" rule as with dollar cost averaging ("buy $100 more stock each month"), the rule under value averaging is to *make the value of your stock holdings go up by $100 (or some other amount) each month.* This is a very simple version of the strategy, to be enhanced later; but the focus on *resulting value* instead of on *investment cost* is the main point. Look at Table 3-1 which shows the same mutual fund prices and investment period that comprised the DCA example in Table 2-1 (page 27).

The example in Table 3-1 shows a value averaging strategy following the rule of making the investment value go up by $100 every month. At the beginning of January 1986, you owned $0 worth of stock, so you had to buy $100 worth of stock (at $4.64) to get 21.55 shares worth $100. Next month, February 1986, the rule says to make the value of your holdings go up by $100 (from $100 to $200), so you must own $200 in stock after your February purchase. Because the new price is $4.38, this means

TABLE 3-1 Example of Value Averaging					
Mutual Fund		VALUE AVERAGING			
Month	Share Price	Total Value	# Shares To Own	# Shares To Buy	($$$) Invested
Jan 86	$4.64	$100	21.55	21.55	($100.00)
Feb 86	$4.38	$200	45.66	24.11	($105.60)
Mar 86	$4.56	$300	65.79	20.13	($91.78)
Apr 86	$4.25	$400	94.12	28.33	($120.39)
May 86	$3.81	$500	131.23	37.12	($141.41)
Jun 86	$3.19	$600	188.09	56.85	($181.36)
Jul 86	$2.99	$700	234.11	46.03	($137.62)
Aug 86	*$3.60*	*$800*	*222.22*	*-11.89*	*$42.81*
Sep 86	$4.70	$900	191.49	- 30.73	$144.44
Oct 86	$4.41	$1,000	226.76	35.27	($155.53)
Nov 86	$4.34	$1,100	253.46	26.70	($115.87)
Dec 86	$4.69	$1,200	255.86	2.41	($11.29)
Jan 87	$5.26	$1,300	247.15	- 8.72	$45.84
Feb 87	$4.54	$1,400	308.37	61.22	($277.95)
Mar 87	$5.38	$1,500	278.81	- 29.56	$159.03
Apr 87	$7.47	$1,600	214.19	- 64.62	$482.71
May 87	$7.39	$1,700	230.04	15.85	($117.14)
Jun 87	$6.31	$1,800	285.26	55.22	($348.44)
Jul 87	$7.07	$1,900	268.74	-16.52	$116.80
Aug 87	$6.48	$2,000	308.64	39.90	($258.56)
Sep 87	$7.07	$2,100	297.03	-11.61	$82.10
Oct 87	$6.96	$2,200	316.09	19.06	($132.67)
Nov 87	$5.05	$2,300	455.45	139.35	($703.74)
Dec 87	$5.80	$2,400	413.79	- 41.65	$241.58
Jan 88	$5.06		Final Value:		$2,094
Avg. Price w/CS			Total Net Cost:		($1,684)
	$5.18		Average Net Cost Per Share:		$4.07
Internal Rate of Return (IRR):					20.1%

Results of value averaging. Recall that in Table 2-1 the IRR for the CS strategy was -0.2%, and the IRR for the DCA strategy was +4.0%.

you must own 45.66 shares at $4.38 to make the value $200. You already own 21.55 shares from January. Thus, you must purchase 24.11 more shares at $4.38, or buy $105.60 worth of shares in February (as shown on the second row of the table). Note that when the share price goes down, as it did here, you will have to spend *more* than $100 to "replace" the lost value. But when the share price goes up, you will have to spend *less* than $100, because capital gains have provided some of your "required" increase in value. This occurs in the next month, March 1986. Due to the rise in share price from $4.38 to $4.56, you would need to invest only $91.78 that month to have your holdings increase by $100 (due to $8.22 of capital gains).

At first glance, the VA strategy may not seem too different from dollar cost averaging, but a look at August 1986 in Table 3-1 reveals one major difference using value averaging: a large upward price swing often results in a *sale* of stock, instead of a purchase. The entire increase in value "dictated" for one month by the value averaging rule could be provided solely by an increase in your portfolio value, given a large enough price rise; then you wouldn't need to provide any additional investment. In the example, after July 1986, you held $700 of stock and needed to increase that value to $800 in August (this row has been italicized in the table). But as a result of the share price increase from $2.99 to $3.60 over that time, your $700 worth of stock was then worth $842.81. You are now $42.81 ahead of your $800 goal, so you get to skim off the extra money by *selling* 11.89 shares ($42.81 worth) that month. Supposedly you would put that money aside—perhaps in a money market fund—to be invested in a later month when the market dips, such as October 1986 in the example above.

Following the value averaging strategy down the rest of the 24-month period, you can see that you would sell shares 8 out of 24 times to keep the value of your holdings increasing at a preset $100/month rate. Value averaging resulted in a net average cost per share of only $4.07 over this period,[2] much lower than the average share cost of $4.85 with dollar cost averaging and the $5.18 average fund price over the period. With value averaging, this occurs because we are not just "buying low," as with dollar cost averaging; we are buying even more than usual when the share price moves exceptionally low. Of course, *low* is defined only relative to the prior period's price. There is certainly no guarantee that this so-called low price will be truly low in any absolute sense, or even relative to future prices.

Also, there is often a tendency with value averaging to sell shares when the share price is high; the best a dollar cost averaging strategy can do is to buy fewer of these expensive shares.

Whereas dollar cost averaging earned you a 4.0% average annual return on your investment over the period, value averaging returned a whopping 20.1% annual return on the same fund over the same time period. Not bad, considering that the final share price ($5.06 versus $4.64) ended up at roughly the same level at which it had started.

Analysis of the above example was extended another 25 months using fund price data through February 1990. The monthly figures are not shown here due to space considerations, but the results are interesting. The final share price on February 15, 1990, was $5.01—still in the same general range as it had been both two and four years earlier. The investment returns still varied widely, even over this longer period: by buying a share per month (CS), the annualized rate of return over the four years was +3.9%; dollar cost averaging improved your return to +6.8%; but value averaging more than doubled that return, yielding an IRR of +13.8%.

The value averaging strategy did quite well with this rather flat[3] but volatile fund. The strategy takes a more extreme response to market dips and rises than does dollar cost averaging. These large responses are not without their problems, as will be discussed in later chapters. Here, though, the return was enhanced greatly by the large purchases at low prices and by the profit taking as shares were sold at generally high prices.

The occasional selling indicated by value averaging rules is probably the single most interesting characteristic of the strategy. Even though neither VA—nor any other strategy—can time market peaks, it still has an interesting timing characteristic. You will sell (or buy far fewer than normal) shares at a market peak because, after all, the price must have gone *up* to have resulted in a market peak. The converse is true with buying more than normal as the market hits its nadir. If you follow its prescription, value averaging forces you to avoid big moves into a peaked market or panic selling at the bottom. That by itself is pretty tasty medicine. Of course, there are problems with selling into a consistent bull market. There can also be tax complications and transaction costs when you sell (these and other complicating issues are covered in Chapter 6). Still, the selling feature is a flexible and potentially useful and rewarding addition to your investment arsenal, particularly because there's so little guidance out there on when to sell, and so little natural tendency to do it after the market has had a good healthy run up.

SHORT-TERM PERFORMANCE

An analysis using historical market data will be shown here, comparing value averaging to dollar cost averaging in a manner that parallels the previous chapter. Both dollar cost averaging and value averaging are used with monthly frequency over the same (one-year or five-year) market period, and the rates of return (IRR) resulting from the two strategies are compared for each period. Value averaging usually provides the highest returns in the stock market over short- and intermediate-term investment periods.

In Table 3-2, the rates of return from using the two strategies are compared for each year of actual stock market history (1926–1991). With dollar cost averaging, $100 is invested at the beginning of each month,[4] and the portfolio is valued on

TABLE 3-2 Comparison of (monthly) DCA vs. VA Rate of Return Over 1-Year Periods					
Year	DCA	VA	Year	DCA	VA
26	18.07%	18.31%	60	12.03%	12.42%
27	36.41%	37.30%	61	20.95%	21.33%
28	48.37%	48.91%	62	4.63%	5.66%
29	- 32.31%	- 30.92%	63	17.48%	17.88%
30	- 45.46%	- 45.82%	64	13.04%	13.19%
31	*- 60.22%*	*- 58.23%*	65	15.52%	15.67%
32	**11.25%**	**25.86%**	66	- 5.74%	- 5.20%
33	**51.30%**	**67.51%**	67	19.55%	20.17%
34	3.11%	4.47%	68	19.62%	20.51%
35	*66.43%*	*65.37%*	69	- 9.71%	- 8.84%
36	34.34%	34.81%	70	*22.45%*	*22.13%*
37	*- 47.67%*	*- 48.21%*	71	13.09%	13.97%
38	43.06%	49.02%	72	17.11%	17.21%
39	16.72%	19.64%	73	-15.64%	-14.38%
40	0.77%	2.79%	74	-26.84%	-24.12%
41	-11.89%	-11.73%	75	15.74%	16.83%
42	*33.65%*	*32.97%*	76	18.44%	18.83%
43	12.08%	13.15%	77	1.45%	1.84%
44	22.49%	22.74%	78	7.46%	9.01%
45	41.75%	42.06%	79	21.67%	22.93%
46	-13.22%	-12.20%	80	39.30%	40.85%
47	8.12%	8.41%	81	- 3.63%	- 2.72%
48	- 0.73%	0.75%	82	*44.85%*	*44.30%*
49	*33.07%*	*32.39%*	83	12.45%	12.93%
50	35.61%	35.64%	84	13.03%	13.73%
51	18.73%	19.32%	85	30.73%	30.86%
52	18.13%	18.39%	86	6.83%	8.32%
53	6.30%	6.50%	87	-21.14%	-18.38%
54	53.14%	53.30%	88	12.74%	13.14%
55	25.71%	26.31%	89	22.71%	23.52%
56	6.41%	7.10%	90	0.12%	1.28%
57	-16.65%	-16.62%	91	26.07%	27.23%
58	49.72%	49.26%	Avg. IRR	12.61%	13.77%
59	11.93%	12.25%			

Investment frequency is monthly. Rate of return is annualized IRR. Italicized entries are for years in which DCA outperformed VA.

the last day of the year, after 12 equal monthly investments. With value averaging, whatever investment (or sale) necessary is made to keep the value increasing at a steady $100 per month until the $1,200 value goal at the beginning of December; final valuation is made at the December 31 market price.

Value averaging had a higher return for 58 of the 66 years analyzed, losing only 8 times. When VA "won," it provided relative returns as much as 16.21 percentage points higher than DCA (in 1933) and averaged 1.24 higher when it won. When VA "lost," its relative returns were never more than -1.06 percentage points lower than DCA (in 1935); the average VA return was only .58% lower than DCA on those few occasions that it lost. Over all 66 years, dollar cost averaging returned an average 12.61%, but value averaging returned an average 13.77%, +1.16% higher. The possible relative gains of the VA strategy seem quite high in both frequency and magnitude, and they compare quite favorably with the risks (relative to DCA). This is especially highlighted by the results for 1932 when the stock market was actually down over 9% from the beginning to the end of that year. The CS strategy had a rate of return of +3.73%, DCA returned +11.25%, and VA returned +25.86% during this bad market year. Monthly figures for 1932 are provided here for the interested reader. The market level is relative to an index of December 31, 1925 = 100, with all dividend returns included in the market value index.

Monthly Market Level Figures for 1932

Beginning of	Market Level	Beginning of	Market Level
January	69.05	July	41.46
February	68.32	August	55.18
March	72.24	September	75.32
April	64.35	October	72.98
May	52.77	November	63.47
June	41.85	December	60.00
		End of Year	**62.66**

The rates of return from using the two strategies for possible (overlapping) 5-year periods of actual stock market history (1926–1930 through 1987–1991) were compared but are not shown here in a full table. Of the 62 possible periods, value averaging had a higher return in 52 of them. The average annualized rate of return with DCA was 10.20%, whereas value averaging returned a 1.13% higher annual average of 11.33%.

Following a "pure" value averaging strategy yields five-year results that are a bit more spotty than one-year results. This begins to highlight a potential problem with the naive rule of making your value go up *by the same amount* every month over longer investment periods. At first that $100 amount is a large increase, but over time it becomes a drop in the bucket. This problem and a simple solution will be discussed in the next section on long-term performance, along with an extended presentation in Chapter 5 of how to set up your "value paths."

With the investment features of more exaggerated buying and the opportunity for selling, value averaging gives you a great chance at enhancing your investment rate of return over short- and medium-term investment periods. Some points brought out in the previous chapter on dollar cost averaging bear mentioning again with respect to our newfound strategy as well. In many years, the strategy used plays very little role in your overall return, compared with your investment's performance. That is, a bad year is a bad year even with value averaging (with limited exceptions, such as 1932). The investment vehicle you choose is far more important to your results than the mechanical rules you follow to invest in it. To that end, it is best to use value averaging with very diversified investments, such as a broad-based mutual fund or, preferably, an index fund. These issues and many more of the minor complexities of value averaging will be highlighted in later chapters.

LONG-TERM PERFORMANCE AND VALUE AVERAGING

Value averaging seems to profit from the peaks and valleys in the market geography. You might suspect that value averaging would perform well over longer investment periods. It can, but not in the "pure" version described above. Value averaging, like its counterpart DCA, fails to take market growth into account in its "linear value path" (adding the *same* amount to value every month). This causes value averaging to fail to keep up with the market and will seriously reduce your investments' total market exposure over long periods. This is contrary to the goal of an accumulation strategy. Suppose you had started three formula plans: a constant share purchase strategy, which is the base case; dollar cost averaging; and value averaging. Suppose further that you started each by investing $1 in January 1926[5] and continued monthly until 1991. You have already seen the figures for the CS and DCA strategies in the previous chapter; now, in the following sections, they are compared with value averaging in tabular format.

Linear, or Fixed-Dollar, Strategies

Table 3-3a shows the results of using the strategies in their purest (and most naive) form. The "fixed-amount" rules are

TABLE 3-3a Comparison of Strategies: 1926–1991 *No Growth for DCA and VA—"Fixed-Amount" Rules*			
Strategy:	CS	Pure DCA	Pure VA
Rate of Return:	11.24%	11.03%	10.80%

Investments were made monthly. Rate of return is annualized IRR of all cash flows. DCA invests, and VA value increases by, the same fixed amount monthly.

taken literally over the 66-year period. Monthly investment under dollar cost averaging is a fixed $1 per month. The value goal under value averaging is strictly linear, with the "required" value increasing by $1 every month. VA performs poorly here, returning only 10.80% compounded annually over the period.

As discussed in the previous chapter, the fixed-amount rules just don't make any sense over a long investment period, due to inflation and to extensive growth in the level of value of the stock market. With dollar cost averaging, the problem was simply that the fixed amount invested buys less and less of the market over time, so that the monthly additions eventually become insignificant. The problem with so-called pure or fixed value averaging is more complex. With a CS strategy, where your investment grows with the market, both your incremental investment (new money) and the value of your previous holdings (old money) are "keeping up," or moving with the market. With a fixed DCA strategy, your $1 incremental investment (new money) becomes insignificant, but at least the value of previously purchased shares (old money) keeps up with the market, as you never sell any of them. But with a fixed value averaging strategy, both the investment increment and the value, which is on a predetermined linear path, will become insignificant over time. Because "old" shares are not left alone (but are subject to being sold under the VA strategy), neither the old nor new money keeps up with the market with VA.

For example, the monthly $1 increase in value results in a portfolio value of only $792 after 66 years. The CS portfolio weighed in at over $422,000 at the same time. Admittedly, much more money was poured into the richer CS strategy, and with value averaging you would actually have taken out substantially more money than you put in.[6] Still, you can see that the fixed, linear, "pure" VA strategy totally loses touch with the reality of sizable increases compounded over time in the market, when viewed in the long run. The $1-a-month increase in value is meaningful at first but becomes insignificant rather quickly. In fact, as market levels rise over time, VA actually acts to consis-

Figure 3-1 RESULTS OF DOLLAR COST AVERAGING

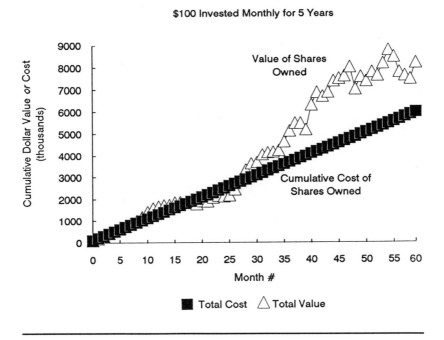

$100 Invested Monthly for 5 Years

The cumulative cost of steady DCA investing increases smoothly; the portfolio value increases randomly, trending well upward.

tently move you *out* of the market, as opposed to accumulating shares in it. It would take less than a decade for this reversal to happen.

Perhaps it is helpful to see graphically the conceptual difference between the dollar cost averaging and value averaging strategies, as shown in Figures 3-1 and 3-2. Each figure shows both the cumulative amount of money invested, and the value of the total portfolio, at each point in time for the given strategy over a five-year period.[7] Figure 3-1 shows the results of dollar cost averaging; Figure 3-2 shows value averaging. The

Figure 3-2 RESULTS OF VALUE AVERAGING

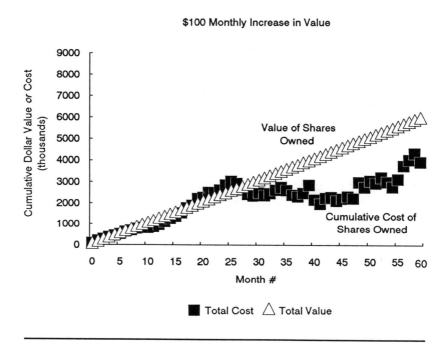

$100 Monthly Increase in Value

With VA, the porfolio value is made to rise at a steady rate; the cumulative amount invested varies randomly.

amount of money put into a DCA strategy (the cumulative cost of shares) goes up smoothly by the fixed amount. The resulting shares increase in value as they accumulate and as the price level of the market rises. Value averaging, on the other hand, does much the opposite in that we force the value of the shares to go up smoothly by the fixed amount. The total amount of money invested in VA (the cumulative cost) then varies randomly, going up when shares need to be purchased, going up a lot when the market is down, and going down if the market increases enough to dictate a sale of shares. Note that with value averaging, there is generally less money invested and a lower final value, as the linear "value path" does not keep pace with the tendency for the stock market (and thus, your own holdings) to grow.

A related problem with value averaging can also be seen in Figure 3-2. The $100-a-month increase in the value goal means a lot when you're just getting started, but later (after some stock is accumulated) it results in very little need for net investment. In the first few months of the accumulation, note how the need for investment (the increase in the "cumulative cost of shares") is close to the desired increase in value. When you don't have many shares yet, almost all of your desired value increase must be new investment; there's just not much action coming from your existing shares. Later on in the accumulation plan, however, you will have built a portfolio that tends to increase in value. By then, much of the $100 increase in value will be provided by the shares already on hand, leaving you little need, on average, for net investment. Eventually, the expected (average) increase in your market holdings will far exceed $100 a month,[8] causing you to *decumulate* shares gradually, putting the brakes on your portfolio growth to stay in line with your slow-moving value goal. Most likely, this is *not* what you want to happen.

Adjusting Strategies for Growth

One possible way to attack this problem is to adjust the value path for inflation. As an example, take a $1,000 "pure" value averaging portfolio after 10 months of $100 value increases. If inflation was one-half percent per month, we could adjust the next month's value goal for inflation. First, take the $1,000 value and give it "growing room" at the inflation rate, to $1,005. Then, the $100 value increment we started out with also could be adjusted for inflation, to $100.50. The next month's value goal could be preset at $1,105.50 instead of just $1,100. Instead of $1,200 the next month's goal would be a value of $1,212.03. The effect *compounds* over time.

We tried this type of inflation adjustment with value averaging, using the same inflation numbers as with dollar cost averaging in the previous chapter. The results of inflation adjusting the DCA and VA strategies, shown in Table 3-3b, are only marginally better than for the unadjusted "pure" strategies. The inflation-adjusted strategies still provide no advantage.

TABLE 3-3b Comparison of Strategies: 1926–1991 Inflation Growth Only for DCA and VA			
Strategy:	CS	DCA + Inflation	VA + Inflation
Rate of Return:	11.22%	11.09%	11.07%

DCA amount to invest adjusted monthly for inflation. VA target value constructed by taking the prior month's value, plus the $1 increment, and then adjusting the total for inflation.

The reason for this disappointing performance has been mentioned a few times before. Even when the value path is adjusted for inflation, the final value with VA is only $8,220 (versus more than $422,000 for CS)—almost no market exposure after 66 years of accumulation. If you expect your investments to outperform inflation (which they had better in the long run), and you set a value path at the inflation rate, then you will actually end up less and less invested in the market over a long period. Your value path will simply fall way behind market growth.

Next, we turn to what would happen if you allowed for sufficient compounding growth in the value path to accumulate the same market exposure with VA as with the CS strategy over the same period. We did this in the previous chapter for DCA and called the adjustment *growth equalization*. The growth-equalized analysis of value averaging is displayed in Table 3-3c.

Some amount of compound growth in the value path, larger than the inflation adjustment, could result in enough money invested through value averaging for that strategy to be comparable to the CS and growth-equalized DCA strategies.

TABLE 3-3c Comparison of Strategies: 1926–1991 *DCA and VA, Growth-Equalized*			
Strategy:	CS	DCA + Growth	VA + Growth
Rate of Return:	11.24%	11.46%	12.56%

Both strategies "growth-equalized" to result in the same (roughly $422,000) final market exposure. DCA amount to invest increased by 0.64% monthly. VA "target value" is the prior month's target increased by 0.79%, plus the increment, starting at $1 and increasing by 0.79% monthly.[9]

Had you adjusted the add-$1-a-month-to-value rule by 0.79% each month (a 9.90% annualized growth rate), you would have ended up with a value goal, and a portfolio value, of about $420,000 by 1991, about the same as with the CS and the growth-equalized DCA strategies. The rate of return on this growth-equalized value averaging strategy would have jumped to 12.56%, much higher than the rate of return from any variation of any strategy we've seen so far.

The main lesson to be repeated here is that the investment formula must somehow keep up with the phenomenal growth in the market over long-term investment periods.

This will be even more true with value averaging, as you will see in the next few chapters. Exactly how to integrate this information into your investment plan with both formula strategies will be covered in Chapters 4 and 5.

SUMMARY

Value averaging has been presented as an alternative method of accumulating market wealth over time. By focusing on a predetermined value goal that increases over time, you take the dollar cost averaging philosophy of "buy more cheap shares" a step further. Returns are generally higher with value averaging, and there is not much downside return risk relative to dollar cost averaging. The features of value averaging make it more flexible but also more complicated than dollar cost averaging. With any of these strategies—but with value averaging in particular—you must be particularly sensitive to keeping pace with long-term market growth to maintain a reasonable market exposure. In the next few chapters, some complications of the value averaging strategies (and of dollar cost averaging) will be discussed, along with an analysis of some recommended ways to use the strategies effectively.

ENDNOTES

1.   The value averaging technique was originally presented in my article, "Value Averaging: A New Approach to Accumulation," *AAII Journal* X, no. 7 (August 1988), 11–14.

2.   This "net cost" figure is perhaps not the most accurate way to report the average cost of shares in the value averaging strategy, because there are both purchases and sales which confounds the accounting. Using the standard "average share" method of accounting for mutual funds, the gross shares purchased break down as follows:

- 215.3 shares, with an average cost basis of $4.26, sold at an average sales price of $6.11;
- 413.79 shares, with an average cost basis of $5.03, remaining at the end of the period.

The $4.03 "net average cost" figure comes from netting out sales—the net amount invested (deducting sales profits), divided by the number of remaining shares (net of sales), comes out to $4.03. But a more common way of tracking the average cost of *all* shares purchased is to just take the weighted average of the quantities above, yielding a gross average purchase price of $4.77 per share. It is still (and must always be) cheaper than with dollar cost averaging. (My thanks to Glenn S. Daily, author of *Low-Load Insurance Products*, International Publishing Corporation, for pointing this out.)

3.   To be fair to the fund in question, it is again noted that this analysis totally leaves out some fairly sizable dividends; also, precious metals funds on average have a much lower expected return than diversified stock funds.

4.   Again, it is noted that the investment is made on the last day of the prior month.

5.   Recall that the price index for stock market value used in this book is based on a "price" of $1 for the beginning of 1926, growing to almost $534 by the end of 1991.

6.   Of course, the IRR calculations take the size and timing of the inflows and outflows into account; in spite of the sizable outflows with the VA strategy, CS still has a higher return by 0.44%.

7.   The underlying "stock" is a typical random simulation of monthly market price data. The simulation process itself is not important here, but is described in detail in Chapter 7.

8.   Using a range of historical and expected returns on the market as discussed in Chapter 1, you could expect this phenomenon to start happening after about 6–10 years, on average.

9.   The 0.64% growth factor for DCA was explained in Chapter 2. The 0.79% growth factor for the VA value path happens to be the right amount of growth to maintain a sufficient market exposure so that value averaging is "as invested in" the market as the other two strategies. Although this figure cannot be ascertained exactly for future periods, a reasonable estimate can be used for your own purposes, as will be explained in the next two chapters.

Investment Goals with Dollar Cost Averaging

4

Considering the discussion in Chapters 2 and 3, it is clear that pursuing a so-called fixed-amount formula investment strategy is not the right way to accumulate market wealth over time. If you fail to take steps to keep pace with long-term market growth, then you will also fail to maintain a reasonable market exposure. Your stock market holdings could dwindle over time as a consequence of adhering to a mathematical formula that wouldn't make sense in the long run. The goal of this chapter on dollar cost averaging (and the next one on value averaging) is to provide the long-term investor with some idea of how investment goals relate to the numbers chosen for formula investment strategies. With a little work, you should be able to use this information to decide, for example, what monthly investment would be necessary to establish a college fund for your newborn, and how to adjust the amounts for later changes.

BACKGROUND

Lump-Sum Investments

The simplest case to start with is a lump-sum investment. Even though this book has focused on accumulation strategies involving a series of investments, each of these series is composed of many little lump-sum investments. Suppose you invested $C (*cash investment*) now at a rate of r% (*rate of return*) for one period. At the end of the period, your future value, V, would be:

$$V = C \times (1+r) \tag{1}$$

For example, if your investment was C = $1,000, the investment period was a month, and the monthly rate of return was r = 1.0% (or 0.01), then your final value a month later would be: V = $1,000 × (1 + 0.01) = $1,010. Note that the rate used must match the period in question. It would not have made much sense to use a 12% *annual* rate directly in the calculation to evaluate the results of investing for only one *month*.

Suppose you allowed an investment to compound over t periods (t stands for *time*). In the second period, not only does your initial investment of C earn interest, but also the interest (r × C) from the first period earns interest. Over 2 periods, this gives you a value, V_2, of:

$$V_2 = V_1 \times (1+r) = C \times (1+r) \times (1+r) = C \times (1+r)^2 \quad (2)$$

For example, if the investment above compounded for 2 months at 1.0% per month, the final value would not be $1,020 (which ignores the compounding) but $1,020.10. The general formula for compounding over t periods is:

$$V_t = C \times (1+r)^t \quad (3)$$

That is, you take the rate of return for a single period, add it to 1 and compound it over the number of periods to get the growth factor; this factor, when multiplied by the initial C investment, yields the final value V_t.

A brief example may be helpful. If a (rather generous) bank says it pays a 12% rate *compounded monthly*, what will your $1,000 grow to in a one-year certificate of deposit? If you said $1,120, you have missed the point. When the bank compounds all of the monthly 1.0% "pieces" of the 12% annual rate, it is actually paying an effective annual yield, or effective rate, of 12.68% over a 12-month period. Using the formula above, the $(1 + r)^t$ part is $(1.01)^{12}$, which is 1.1268, so your final value V grows to 1.1268 times your investment C, or a 12.68% increase—$1,126.82 in this case. Calculating $(1.01)^{12}$, taking 1.01

to the 12th power, is easy as long as your calculator has an exponent or power key—this key normally has y^x on it. Just enter 1.01, then hit the y^x key, then enter 12, and hit the " = " key. This example shows how to "annualize" a monthly rate of return, as is done consistently throughout this book. A 1.0% monthly return is equivalent to a 12.68% (not a 12%) annualized return.[1]

Using the Formula

By taking the formula **(3)** above and putting in a value goal, V_t for some point in the future, you could solve for the lump-sum cash investment, $C, needed now to achieve that goal. Let's look at the example of a new mother who figures she'll need $100,000 to send her child to college in 18 years. If she can earn an effective annual return of 10% per year, how much must she set aside today for her one-shot investment to provide the funds she needs later? We'll look at three possibilities, considering taxes differently in each.

First, if—for some strange reason—taxes are not an issue, then the equation is: $100,000 = C \times (1.10)^{18}$. The quantity 1.10^{18} equals 5.56, so that $1 grows to $5.56; thus, we say that the "growth factor" at 10% over 18 years is 5.56. Dividing that into $100,000, the required cash investment (C) is $17,986 today.

Second, suppose the education account here was fully tax-deferred,[2] such as a Keogh plan or fully deductible IRA. Upon withdrawal, when the amount taken out would be taxed, the mother would need $149,254 in 18 years if she were in the 33% tax bracket[3] to yield $100,000 after taxes. Putting this larger figure in the formula in the place of $100,000 gives a required $C of $26,844.64 invested in the account today (using the same 18-year, 10% growth factor. In the 28% tax bracket, the required amount would be $24,980 today.

Third, take the case of a fully taxed investment earning 10% before taxes, which is 7.2% (28% bracket) or 6.7% (33% bracket) after taxes. Now the formula for the 28% bracket investor would be: $100,000 = C \times (1.072)^{18}$. The after-tax compound rate is 7.2%, in place of 10%. In the 28% tax bracket, the after-tax growth factor is 3.495. That means the mother would need $28,608 today to fund the expected college costs. If in the higher tax bracket, she would need $31,120 today.

The main plot of these examples was figuring out numbers for current investments based on future needs. However, the examples also contain a subplot on the benefits of tax deferral you should take note of.

Because most people don't like fiddling with formulas and exponents, many calculators and all spreadsheets will now solve such calculations for you quickly. Any financial calculator generally requires that you give it any 3 variables, and then it will calculate the 4th one, which you must designate. How you would solve the first example above using a financial calculator is shown in the box on page 61.

Annuities: Periodic Investments

Instead of a single lump-sum investment, we will now consider ongoing periodic investments, generally referred to as *annuities.* Suppose the mother in the preceding example doesn't have the $18,000–$30,000 required now to fund her child's education. How much money would she need to set aside at the end of each year over the next 18 years to meet her goal? To determine this, let $C now be the periodic investment amount that she makes at the end of each period. How much money will that series of investments of $C grow into over time? Letting V_t be the final value after t periods, the annuity formula is:

$$V_t = C_{end} \times \frac{1}{r} \left[(1+r)^t - 1 \right] \tag{4}$$

FINANCIAL CALCULATOR SOLUTION

Jan estimates that in 18 years she will need $100,000 to send Chris to college. She expects to earn 10% per year and pay no taxes at all. How much should she set aside today?

Solution Steps

Although each calculator model is different, they all involve the same basic steps. Read your manual to be sure these steps will work on your model.

1. Make sure your calculator is in the finance mode; clear all settings.
2. Enter 100,000 into the *FV* key.
3. Enter 10 into the *i*, *int*, or *r* key.
4. Enter 18 into the *n* or *t* key.
5. "Compute" the *PV* key (this step may involve pressing a separate *Compute* key prior to pressing the *PV* key).

The display should read 17,986, or some number very close to that. If not, check these steps against your manual.

Answer: $17,986

Thus, putting in 0.1 (10%) for *r* and 18 for *t*, we get an annuity growth factor (all the terms to the right of the multiplication sign) of 45.6. This means that after 18 annual end-of-year $1 investments at 10%, we'll have a final total of $45.60. Dividing through by this factor, we can solve for the required $*C* of $2,193. Thus, she needs to invest $2,193 at the end of each of the next 18 years to reach the $100,000 goal. Luckily, financial calculators and computers can do this for you, as is shown in the box on page 62.

What if you had not needed to make end-of-year investments but instead were ready to start right away? It is very simple to adjust the formula for beginning-of-year investments instead of end-of-year ones. Because the "value" of moving each investment up in time by a year is an extra year's interest

---

FINANCIAL CALCULATOR SOLUTION—ANNUITY

Jan estimates that in 18 years she will need $100,000 to send Chris to college. She expects to earn 10% per year and pay no taxes at all. How much should she set aside at the end of each of the 18 years?

Solution Steps

1. Make sure your calculator is in the finance mode; clear all settings.
2. Enter 100,000 into the *FV* key.
3. Enter 10 into the *i*, *int*, or *r* key.
4. Enter 18 into the *n* or *t* key.
5. "Compute" the *PMT* key (this step may involve pressing a separate *Compute* key prior to pressing the *PMT* key).

The display should read 2,193, or some number very close to that. If not, check these steps against your manual.

Answer: $2,193 per year

---

throughout, we can just add that interest into the final growth factor, increasing the final $45.60 growth factor by 10%, or multiplying it by 1.10, to get a factor of 50.16, yielding a required beginning-of-year investment of $1,994 over the next 18 years. You could get the same answer by dividing the $2,193 end-of-year investment by 1.10 to get $1,994, which makes perfect sense, because if you had $1,994 at the *beginning* of the year, you would have (at 10%) $2,193 at the *end* of the year. The following formula for using beginning-of-period investments is the same as **(4)** above, multiplied by $(1 + r)$:

$$V_t = C_{beg} \times \frac{1+r}{r} [(1+r)^t - 1] \qquad (5)$$

Remember that the distinction is not the beginning or end of the *calendar* period but is relative to *today*—do you make the first $C investment right away, or do you wait one investment period before doing so?

What about handling a different period, such as monthly investments? Then the monthly period would have to go along with a monthly rate of return. What monthly return would equate to a 10% annual effective rate? It works out to 0.7974% monthly (that is, $1.007974^{12} = 1.10$). Now we have that rate for r and $18 \times 12 = 216$ months for t. Using the end-of-month formula, the calculation results in a growth factor of 571.838 times the monthly investment, or a requirement of $174.87 at the end of each month over 18 years. The beginning-of-month amount would be $173.49. See if you can get these values using your calculator.

Dollar Cost Averaging and Annuities

These annuity formulas can help you relate your investment goals to the "fixed amount" you need to invest in a so-called pure dollar cost averaging strategy. Because dollar cost averaging does invest a fixed dollar amount every period, it is an annuity. Therefore, if you were going to dollar cost average $100 at the end of every month over a period of 20 years, and if you expected an average compound monthly increase of 1.0% each month (12.68% effective annually), you would accumulate $98,925[4] at the end of the 240 months.

READJUSTING THE INVESTMENT PLAN

Of course, solving for C as above and investing $$C$ each period to achieve your goal works only if you end up actually getting the rate of return, r, that you projected as an input to the formula. When you are invested in any risky investment—such as the stock market—there are no return guarantees. All we can do to start out is use some *expected return* on the market, as discussed in Chapter 1. For instance, we could assume that the random market return will be centered on average (that is, *expected* to be) at a 12.68% compound annual return (or, 1.0% compound monthly return). But it is unlikely that this is exactly the return you will achieve. So if you intend to follow a (C) fixed-amount dollar cost averaging strategy, what can you do if your investment results turn out different than you expected?

The Readjustment Process

One way to approach this problem is to start out as above and then occasionally readjust the fixed investment amount to reflect where you are relative to your goal. Look at the four logical steps in the procedure to determine the investment amount (C):

1. Determine V_t, your investment goal for time t;
2. Determine the r, or expected rate of return, that you *reasonably* expect to get on average, after taxes;
3. Use the annuity formula or a financial calculator or computer to calculate the required (C) fixed-dollar per-period investment to achieve your goal in step 1 at the rate in step 2 in t periods;
4. After several periods, recalculate the new amount required, using your actual value today as the starting point for the remainder of your investment time available. Continue the investment program with the *new* fixed amount for C (this will take a couple of steps, unless you have a financial calculator).

This is an incredibly useful approach you can use to keep your target in sight even with a risky investment and a constantly moving investment target. We'll go through an example of this process, ignoring taxes (or assuming that investment returns are "after-tax") so as to keep the numbers a bit easier. Let's look at a 20-year monthly dollar cost averaging plan where we readjust every year to retarget the goal.

1. Suppose you'll need $100,000 in 20 years.
2. We expect a rate of return on our investments of 1.0% monthly (12.68% annually).
3. Using formula **(4)**—end-of-month—we calculate that the monthly investment required ($C) is $101.09. (We'll use $100 instead; because we are going to readjust every year, we can "catch up" on the few missing dollars later.)

Based on our initial calculations, then, we set off on our investment plan, investing $100 at the end of each month. If the market moves at a 12.68% annual clip, we expect to have $1,268.25 accumulated at the end of 12 months. But suppose the market has a year like 1990 and the value of our portfolio after a year is only $1,100 (a huge loss of -1.6% compounded monthly, or -17.6% annually). We are now behind our expected progress ($1,268.25) toward our $100,000 goal by quite a bit. It is clear that our new $C, or monthly investment amount, must be over $100—in fact, over the original $101.09 we calculated.

If you are careful, you can calculate the new $C amount for the remaining 19 years (228 months) in two steps. Think of the $1,100 you've already accumulated as one pot of money that will grow over time to help you achieve your goal. Think of the (new) $C annuity you're going to contribute over the remaining 228 months as a separate second pot of money. You know that, both growing at r (still 1.0%/month), they will have to add up to $100,000 in another 228 months—the remaining 19 years. So simply calculate what the first pot of money will grow to in the time remaining (using equation **(3)**), deduct it from the $100,000 total goal, and then calculate the $C needed to make up the difference with the second pot of money (with equation **(4)** or **(5)**). Remember that there are now only 228 months (not 240) remaining. We calculate that the $1,100 is expected to grow to $10,633:

$$V_{Pot1} = Pot1 \times (1+r)^t = \$1,100 \times (1.01)^{228} = \$10,633 \quad (6)$$

This means we still need to contribute a second pot of money that eventually grow to $89,367, the amount needed to add up to our $100,000 goal. Using the annuity formula (4), and $89,367 as the required value, V_t, we solve for C:

$$\$89,367 = C \times \frac{1}{0.01} [(1.01)^{228} - 1] \quad (7)$$

$$\$89,367 = C \times 866.66 \quad \rightarrow \quad \$C = \$103.12 \quad (8)$$

From here on, if the market performs as expected, we will need to make a monthly investment of $103.12 over the next 19 years to reach our goal. You could immediately change your monthly fixed amount to $103.12, or maybe just $103 or even $104; or you could choose not to adjust it at all and wait until next year and perhaps make a bigger adjustment. Whatever you do, in another year or so you should readjust again, calculating a new investment amount. (See solution in the box on page 67.)

Flexibility

To further show the flexibility of this approach, we'll take another look at this example while making it more realistic and a bit more complex. Suppose we are now 10 years into our 20-year time frame. When we started, we figured to have $23,255 by this time (to be on target with our $100,000 goal). But our investments have not fared quite as well as expected, and we have a portfolio value of only $22,000 with 10 years remaining. The latest adjustment to $C has had us investing $122 per month during our tenth year. Due to excessive tuition increases,

---

FINANCIAL CALCULATOR SOLUTION—READJUSTMENT

You have $1,100 so far, and you expect a 1% monthly return. You need $100,000 in 19 more years. How much do you need to invest at the end of each month from here on?

Most calculators will let you solve this problem all in 1 step. There are now 5 variables, with only 1 unknown: *PMT*.

Inputs

N	228
i	1% (most calculators take a 1, some a 0.01)
PV	-1,100
FV	100,000

Compute Output

PMT	Press the right keys to "Compute PMT"; the answer of $103.12 should appear.

---

our final goal of $100,000 must be adjusted upward to $110,000. Also, our expected after-tax rate of return is decreased—due to some "revenue enhancement" in the tax codes—so that where we had expected a monthly return of 1.0%, tax increases reduced this compound monthly return to 0.9% (11.35% annually). Now what can we do to achieve our goal?

The two-pot process can handle all of these changes. The only figure from "past history" that will be relevant is the actual current value of $22,000, the first pot. In 120 months remaining, at a new rate of 0.9% it will grow by a factor of 2.93 to $64,471:

$$V_{Pot1} = Pot1 \times (1+r)^t = \$22,000 \times (1.009)^{120} = \$64,471$$

That leaves us with a gap of $45,529 ($110,000 - $64,471)—the value that our second pot of money must build to over the next

10 years. Letting \$45,529 be the final value, V_t, in the annuity formula **(4)** and using the 0.9% rate, we solve for the new \$C:

$$\$45,529 = \$C \times 214.50, \text{ yielding a value for } \$C \text{ of:}$$

$$\$C = \$45,529 \div 214.50 = \$212.26$$

If we expect to achieve our goal in this scenario, we will have to raise our monthly investment to about \$212. The financial calculator can handle this problem in one step, as shown in the box below.

There are two important points here. First, this *readjustment* method is incredibly flexible and can be used to realign your investment performance with your ultimate investment goals on a periodic basis. Second, bad news in the later stages of an accumulation program will have a significant impact on how much you have to increase your investment to make up the difference. Here we had three pretty big pieces of bad news, and the effect was substantial. Because of this, it may be good

---

FINANCIAL CALCULATOR SOLUTION—
10-YEAR READJUSTMENT

You now have \$22,000 and expect only a 0.9% monthly return. You need \$110,000 in 10 more years. How much do you need to invest at the end of each month from here on?

Inputs

N	120
i	0.9
PV	-22,000
FV	110,000

Compute Output

PMT   Press the right keys to "Compute PMT"; the answer of approximately \$212.26 should appear.

in the initial years of an accumulation plan to be a bit conservative in your assumptions. Also, after a really good investment year, you could let your value stay ahead of target instead of readjusting. You wouldn't have to adjust your investment amount downward—after all, you've already gotten used to setting aside a certain amount each period.

Down-Shifting Investment Risk

A wise alternative, if you are ahead of target, is to shift some assets into less risky (but thus less lucrative) investment vehicles. If you shifted half of your investment[5] out of a medium-risk stock fund (monthly return of, say, 1.0%) into government bonds (0.6% monthly return), then your average expected future return would slip from 1.0% monthly to 0.8% monthly. Now recalculate the two pots of money into the future at the lower 0.8% rate to see if you can still achieve your goal with this lower (but safer!) rate of return. If not, then either shift less money into the bonds, or perhaps increase your monthly investment. The reason for the shift should be clear. Investing in the stock market is great for long-term goals, but as you approach your goal-spending requirement (for example, as tuition comes due), you most likely do not want your entire college fund sitting in a risky mutual fund. A bad market result could cause you to suddenly come up very short of funds at the last minute. Over time, it makes sense to gradually shift more funds from risky to less risky investments, realizing that your expected return will go down as you do this.

Here's an example of how this might work. Suppose you are in the 28% tax bracket and you think that you will need about $100,000 after taxes withdrawn from a tax-deferred retirement account in 20 years. You will be taxed upon withdrawal, so you figure you really need $140,000 in the account to clear $100,000 after taxes. Because 20 years is a long time from now, you decide to use a no-load stock index mutual fund as your sole investment vehicle and conservatively use a 1.0% monthly expected rate of return for initial calculations. Thus, you would need to invest about *$141* per month to come up with $140,000 in the account after 240 months.

Ten years later, you find that your stock fund investment has progressed at a compound 1.2% monthly rate (15.4% yearly), a bit higher than you had planned. If you had been investing $141 per month, this would have given you an accumulated wealth of $37,420. By either going through the two-pot method or by directly solving with a financial calculator, you find that you need invest only about $72 per month over the remaining 10 years to achieve your goal at a 1.0% monthly expected rate of return. At a 0.9% rate of return you would need to invest $142; and at a 0.8% return, $213 monthly would be required.

Suppose that "riskless" investments (10-year government zero-coupon bonds for our purpose) are yielding 7.5%, or 0.6% monthly. If we had half our portfolio in stocks (at 1.0%) and half in bonds (at 0.6%), then we would *expect* an average 0.8% return in the future, and would bear only half the risk that we now do, invested totally in stocks. If we shifted only one-quarter of the value of our portfolio into bonds the average expected return would be 0.9%.

So which of these options do we pursue? Keeping your portfolio all in stocks and reducing the monthly investment by half to $72 certainly does not seem to be a very prudent course of action. You could shift one-quarter of your fund into bonds and then keep making the same $142 monthly investment. But you really ought to be able to invest more dollars 10 years into the plan (as opposed to at the beginning), simply due to inflation if nothing else. So a reasonable alternative would be to shift half of your portfolio into bonds while increasing your monthly investment from $141 to $213. This substantially reduces your risk of missing your target over the last 10 years. Of course, there are unlimited options; playing these what-if games should allow you to find one that you are most comfortable with.

One sensible alternative approach, which will be the topic of the remainder of this chapter, is to increase the investment amount for dollar cost averaging for market growth and/or inflation.

GROWTH-ADJUSTED DOLLAR COST AVERAGING

So far, we have only analyzed how to set and adjust investment amounts with a "fixed-dollar" or "pure" dollar cost averaging strategy. A fixed-dollar strategy may be viable over a few years; but for the reasons outlined in Chapter 2, it doesn't really make sense for a long-term investment period. If you had been committing $50 each month to an investment program in 1970, it is very likely that over time the amount you can invest has increased due to inflation or to growth in your real income. By the same token, if you are planning on a $200 monthly investment starting now, it isn't rational to expect that you'll keep that amount fixed as inflation eats away at its purchasing power and as the value of the market moves up over time. This section examines a *growth-adjusted* variation of dollar cost averaging, so that you can plan for some increase in your periodic investments over time. The advantage of this growth is that you can start with less of an investment (because the starting amount will grow) and average out your risk exposure more smoothly over time. When you invest exactly $100 a month over a 20-year period, you've really invested *far more* during the first few years than in the last, due to the decline in purchasing power of the $100. But if you start investing only $50 a month, gradually increasing that amount over the entire period to perhaps $200 or so, your "real" investment remains steadier over time.

There are two forms of growth to be concerned with in a dollar cost averaging strategy, one of which was discussed in the previous section. Our current portfolio will increase (on average we hope) at an expected rate of return we have termed r. Now we will allow for a second form of growth—an increasing periodic investment. Instead of a $\$C$ fixed amount invested each period, we will now cause C to grow at a growth rate, which we term g. For example, if we start with $C = \$100$ and choose a growth rate of $g = 0.5\%$ in a monthly investment program, after a year our monthly investment would increase to $\$106.17$; after 10 years, we would invest $\$181.94$. Of course, you wouldn't have to actually increase your investment every month; that would be inconvenient for the many people with automatic transfer of a constant monthly sum. In that case, you could adjust the amount annually[6] or at some other convenient interval.

Exact Formula

The formula for the value after t periods, V_t, of growth-adjusted DCA investments that start at $\$C$ and then are increased at rate g, invested at a rate of return of r per period, is:

Exact Growth-Adjusted DCA Formula

$$V_t = C_{end} \times \frac{1}{r-g} [(1+r)^t - (1+g)^t] \qquad (9)$$

This formula applies if $r > g$, and if investments are made at the end of the period. If investments start right away, then you can multiply the right side of this equation by $(1 + r)$, as with the beginning-of-period annuity formula (5).

Let's apply this equation to our 20-year investment example with a $\$100,000$ goal. Recall that the fixed amount ($\$C$) for dollar cost averaging was $\$101.09$ each month. Suppose that our investor, who was previously going to invest a fixed $\$101.09$ every month, is now willing to increase the initial investment amount by 0.5% monthly, an annual increase of 6.17%. How much would the initial monthly investment, $\$C$, have to be to achieve the $100,000 goal? Using a final value of $100,000 in 240 months in equation **(9)** with $g = 0.005$ and $r = 0.01$, we get:

$$\$100{,}000 = C \times \frac{1}{0.01 - 0.005} \left[(1.01)^{240} - (1.005)^{240} \right] \quad (10)$$

$$\$100{,}000 = C \times 1{,}516.5 \quad \rightarrow \quad \$C = \$65.94 \quad (11)$$

With a growth adjustment, the growth factor of a $1 monthly investment plan (growing at 0.5%) is 1,516.5, as opposed to only 989 with no growth. Thus, we can satisfy our $100,000 goal with an initial monthly investment of only $65.94,[7] as long as we increase it by one-half percent per month, and get a 1.0% average monthly rate of return on our investment. This $65.94 amount for growth-adjusted dollar cost averaging compares with the $101.09 fixed amount required under pure dollar cost averaging. By the final month, the monthly investment will have increased to $218.27, after 20 years of increases. With the growth-adjusted strategy, you pay less now and more later.

    The formula **(9)** we just used can be simplified by looking at the special case where our two growth variables are equal ($g = r$). That is, we increase our investment by the amount required to "keep up" with the expected average increase on the market. In this case, the final value after t periods[8] can be derived,[9] resulting in:

Single Growth Factor DCA Formula

$$V_t = C \times t \times (1+R)^t \quad (12)$$

where R is the common variable representing both the rate of return (r) and the growth rate of the investment (g); thus $R = r = g$. It almost looks like the lump-sum formula **(3)**, except that the $C investment is multiplied by t, the number of periods. This is a very important and extremely versatile formula, as you will see during the remainder of this chapter.

Applying this formula to the example above, we can see what initial monthly investment would be required if we were willing to increase it at the same 1.0% monthly rate that is also the expected rate of return on our portfolio value. Using equation **(12)** with $R = 0.01$ yields:

$$\$100{,}000 = C \times 240 \times (1.01)^{240} \tag{13}$$

$$\$100{,}000 = C \times 2{,}614.2 \quad \rightarrow \quad \$C = \$38.25 \tag{14}$$

With a full 1.0% growth adjustment, the growth factor of a $1 initial monthly investment plan is 2,614.2. Thus, we can satisfy our $100,000 goal with an initial monthly investment of only $38.25, as long as we increase it by 1.0% per month and also get a 1.0% monthly rate of return on our investment. Of course, with the sizable rate of increase we've chosen, your final monthly payments in year 20 would exceed $400.

Approximate Formula

This formula **(12)** is very easy to work with, particularly when compared to equation **(9)**. However, the formula applies only if $g = r$; for lower, more reasonable levels of increase, or $g <$ r, equation **(9)** applies exactly. But it turns out that you can always use equation **(12)** to get a very close approximation, even when the two growth rates (g and r) are different, simply by averaging them. You can use this approximate formula with the average of the growth rates in place of R. Note that the $\approx$ or "squiggly" equal sign means *approximately equal to.*

Approximate Growth-Adjusted DCA Formula

$$V_t \;\approx\; C \times t \times (1+R)^t \quad where \;\; R = \frac{r+g}{2} \tag{15}$$

For example, let's go back to the first growth-adjusted dollar cost averaging scenario, where we started with an initial monthly investment of $65.94, increased it by $g = 0.5\%$ per month, and expected a rate of return of $r = 1.0\%$ per month on our investments, yielding $100,000 in 20 years. We had to use equation **(9)** to come up with the $C = 65.94 figure. We can solve for the approximate C amount using equation **(15)**, where R is the average of r and g, or 0.75% in this example:

$$\$100,000 \approx C \times 240 \times (1.0075)^{240} = 1{,}442.2\ C$$

This gives us an approximate growth factor of 1,442.2 (compared with 1,516.5 exact), yielding an approximate value for C of $69.34 (compared with $65.94 exact). The approximation is usually fairly close, particularly if r and g are fairly close. For example, using a $g = 0.8\%$ increase rate, which is close to $r = 1.0\%$, yields an *exact* initial investment requirement of $C = 48.50. By using the approximation formula, with $R = 0.9\%$ (average), you get an approximate value of $48.52 for C. Even if the formula does produce a number that is several dollars off, this won't really matter if you periodically readjust your investment plan to account for market performance. If you care about reaching your investment goal, you should be readjusting periodically anyway. And remember, if $g = r$, the formula is not an approximation, but is exact.

Readjusting the DCA Plan

The market's performance is random, so our actual portfolio value will stray from our target path whenever the market does better or worse than expected. If we do not adjust our investment plan after a bad market year, then either the market will have to do better than expected in the future or we will fail to achieve our investment goal. As with the *pure* dollar cost averaging strategy, though, we can readjust the *growth-adjusted* dollar cost averaging over time to keep us on track. But now there are *two* variables we can work with to adjust our monthly investments—$C and g, the amount of our monthly investment and the rate of increase in that amount, respectively. Let's take a look at an example of readjustment in the 20-year investment plan, using the same two-pot technique seen earlier in the chapter. After that, I'll show you a shortcut.

Assume you invested the "exact" $C amount of $65.94 with a 0.5% increase each month, with the goal of $100,000 of value after 20 years. If in the first year you had a great bull market that doubled your expectations (2% monthly return instead of the 1% you expected), you would have an actual value of $908.06 after 12 months instead of the $859 you anticipated. Your initial monthly investment of $65.94,[10] growing at 0.5% per month, would by now be $70.00. The first pot of money, the $908.06 already on hand, is expected to grow (at $r = 1.0\%$) to $8,778 over the remaining 19 years, leaving the need for a second pot of money of $91,222 to sprout from our remaining growing monthly investments over time. If we change nothing and continue with the present plan, we will end up with too much money (actually, being conservative like this early in a plan may not be a bad idea). To get exactly $100,000, we can change our plan to put in a bit less money over the remaining years. There are two ways to accomplish this: either adjust our current $C (option A) or our future rate of increase, g (option B). Option A would use equation (9) with $r = 1.0\%$ and $g = 0.5\%$, $t = 228$ months, and $V = \$91,222$, and solve for the required C. The growth factor on the right side of (9) is 1,309.7, yielding a solution of $C = \$69.65$. You could proceed as if your current investment amount had dropped from $70.00 to this $69.65, using 0.5% increase per month from this newly calculated level.[11]

Option B, the more natural option in my opinion, would be to adjust the rate of increase in your amount invested (g) using the current ($70.00) value for $C. Unfortunately, this is really hard to do with formula **(9)**; by trial and error, you find that you can reduce the value for g to a 0.49% (from 0.50%) increase per month. No matter which way you solved it, this difference (reduce $C by $.35 or cut 0.01% from g) is so inconsequential that you would likely make no readjustment this year, waiting instead until next year's readjustment before considering doing anything different.

   If this seems like a lot of work to you, I'd have to agree. But I've worked out a shortcut method for calculating an approximate readjustment that, although it still involves a little calculator button pressing, is much easier. Keep in mind that the goal here is to solve for a readjusted growth factor by which to increase the monthly investment in the future. We go back to the approximation formula, equation **(15)**, where we take R to be the average of r and g. Now if we designate T to be the total number of investment periods from start to finish (240 months in this example), and designate t as the number of periods already elapsed (12 months in this example), then we can develop an approximate formula for R_f, a new variable that is the *future* adjustment, or average of r and g_f, where g_f is defined as the future required increase in $C (the corresponding new version of g). This R_f will solve:

$$\frac{V_T - V_t \times (1+r)^{T-t}}{C_t \times (T-t)} \approx (1+R_f)^{T-t} \quad \text{where } R_f = \frac{r+g_f}{2} \quad (16)$$

or equivalently:

$$\frac{\text{Target Value} - \text{Exp. Value of Pot1}}{\text{Last Month's Investment} \times \text{\# periods left}} = (1+R_f)^{\text{\# periods left}} \quad (17)$$

The notation C_t is the monthly investment $C at time t (e.g., having grown already for t periods). This method simply combines the two-pot technique of readjustment with the approximation formula, equation **(15)**. In the numerator, you 'take your current pot of money—V_t—and compound it at the expected rate of return over the remaining periods to get the expected future value of the first pot. Deduct this from the total money you will need to arrive at the future value of the money you will need from the second pot—from growing future monthly investments. Once you solve for R_f you find the future adjustment factor, g_f, that averages out to that R_f when combined with r, our expected return on the market.

For example, assume you used the approximate starting value of $69.34 for the monthly investment base of our 20-year, $100,000 plan. The planned values for r and g were 1.0% and 0.5%, respectively, so that R was 0.75%. After 10 years, using the approximation formula (15), you would have expected a value of $20,400; your current monthly investment by the end of year 10 would have risen to $126.16. But the market did better than expected by going up at a 14.1% compound annual rate, so that we now have a value of $22,000 instead. Taking the $22,000 forward the remaining 10 years at a 1.0% return per month, we get a future value of $72,609, which we deduct from the $100,000 goal, thus creating a need to raise an additional $27,391 from future monthly investments. Dividing this by the current monthly investment C_t of $126.16, and by the 120 periods remaining, gives a value of 1.8093 for the quantity $(1 + R_f)^{T-t}$, where $T - t$ is 120. Taking the 120th root (that is, raising to the 1/120 power on the calculator) and subtracting the 1 gives the approximate solution for the R_f factor of 0.4953%. We know that the average of the rate of return r (which is 1.0%) and the new future growth factor g_f is 0.4953%, so the approximate solution for g_f is -0.01%, or zero, for all practical purposes:

$$g_f \approx 2 \times R_f - r \approx 2 \times 0.4953\% - 1.0000\% \approx -0.0094\% \quad (18)$$

This means that you would readjust your rate of *increase* in C down from +0.5% monthly to 0%, or no change—you'd hold steady at a $126.16 monthly investment. This is just an approximation; it turns out not to be a bad one. If you were to do this, the second pot of monthly investments in years 11–20 would be expected to end up with a final value of $29,022 (using the exact formula, equation **(9)**). Your final portfolio value would be $101,630, just a little bit more than our goal.

In case you want to try one of these calculations on your own to check your understanding, try the next annual adjustment. Continue to use a $126.16 monthly investment, but in year 11 assume the market turns down, so that the total portfolio value at the end of month 132 is still only $22,000. You should get $R_f = 0.892\%$, and a new growth factor of $g_f = +0.785\%$; your next monthly investment would go up to $127.15 and continue to increase by 0.785% monthly. If you are considering using a spreadsheet program to do your periodic readjusting, please see the Appendix to Chapter 4 on page 83 for an exact solution to this problem, a copy of the spreadsheet used to solve it, and a listing of all formulas so that you can construct your own spreadsheet if you so desire.

Just as with so-called pure dollar cost averaging, this readjustment approach is totally flexible. If your final goal changes, or the expected return on the market changes, or even if you want to restart your C (monthly amount) over at some different level, this approach can easily handle it. With nearly any investment plan, you are trying to hit a moving target while bouncing over bumpy terrain—you just have to keep aiming until you close in and hit your target. You would probably readjust your growth factor every year or so. Readjusting your portfolio as described in this chapter is crucial to achieving your investment goals.

An important point brought up earlier in this chapter bears mentioning again. It is wise to gradually down-shift your risk level as the time of your investment goal approaches. Start with conservative estimates of how well your investments will do, and take opportunities to shift to lower-return, lower-risk investments later in the plan if you are doing well and if it suits your purpose. You will then be at less risk of missing your final investment target.

SUMMARY

This material has been a bit complex, but most investors skilled with a calculator or a spreadsheet should find little trouble grinding through the calculations once a year or so if they follow the examples and use the formulas provided. With these tools in hand, the millions of investors who dollar cost average can now get some idea of how much investment will be required to achieve their goals, and how to change that investment over time in response to a changing investment climate.

A full case-study example that covers all of these issues is included in Chapter 11.

ENDNOTES

1.   For simplicity, many of the "rates" that you see on financial instruments such as loans, mortgages, credit cards, and the like, are *not* quoted in *effective,* or truly *annualized,* terms. The typical "19.8% APR" quoted on a credit card is really 1.65% (19.8% ÷ 12) monthly, which equates to an effective annual rate of 21.70% on the initial balance. Laws concerning the quoting of APR accept this camouflage of "true" annualized rates for the benefit of standardization to avoid confusion.

2.   On a *fully* tax-deferred investment where you get a current deduction for your investment (such as a deductible IRA or Keogh), both the principal and interest are taxable later upon withdrawal. This is opposed to a *partially* tax-deferred investment, such as an annuity, where your investment is already post-tax (no current deduction), so that only the income on the investment is taxed later at withdrawal. The latter type of investment is tougher to analyze due to the tax code.

3.   Although the top bracket has been reduced to 31%, the deduction phaseouts cause the effective rates to vary at levels above 31%; so the 33% rate is still reasonable for upper-income investors. These rates are expected to rise for some taxpayers under the Clinton Administration.

4.   Or you would have had $99,915 (1.0% more) if you had made the investments at the beginning of the month.

5.   You would also put half of future additions into each investment to make this work out exactly. But then, if you are readjusting each year, there's no need to be exact.

6.   You might really want to make annual adjustments in mid-year. By making no adjustments for six months, you are six months behind; you can now get six months "ahead," and end up investing the right amount on balance. Over time, end-of-year adjustments will leave you about one-half of $r\%$ "behind schedule," or—in this case—about 3% under target.

7.   This initial value is actually for month 0, or right now, even though we are not investing until a month later. Applying the necessary $g = 0.5\%$ growth rate to this figure, our investment for month 1 (our first real investment) is really $66.27.

8.   This formula applies to investments starting one period out. If investments start right away, then multiply the formula by the quantity $(1 + r)$ to account for the extra period.

9.   The derivation of this formula is beyond the scope of this book.

10.   Actually, $66.27 in month 1, as noted above.

11.   Coincidentally, your next month's investment (a 0.5% increase) would be $70.00—so you would just stay at $70 for two months in a row.

Appendix to Chapter 4

Constructing a DCA Readjustment Spreadsheet

The following spreadsheet shows the exact solution, using Equation **9**, of the last DCA readjustment example from Chapter 4 on page 79. After 11 years, having accumulated $22,000, you now have 9 years (108 months) left to earn $100,000 with DCA. Your last monthly investment was $126.16, and you expect a 1.0% average monthly rate of return on your investment. *By how much must you increase each future monthly investment to achieve your goal? (Find g.)*

Lotus 1-2-3 Spreadsheet, DCA Readjustment Program

CELL	A	B	C	D	E	F	G	H
1				*6 INPUTS:*		AMOUNT TO INVEST		
2				========	in #	months	$C	
3	Final Investment Goal:			$100,000		1	$127.17	next mo.
4	Value, Current Holdings			$22,000		2	$128.19	
5	Exp. Rtn. Investment (*i*):			1.00%		3	$129.21	
6	Incr., DCA Amount (*g*):			*0.80%*	<——	4	$130.25	
7	Amount Last Investment:			$126.16		5	$131.29	
8	# Months Remaining:			108		6	$132.34	
9				========		7	$133.40	
10	Expected Value of Pot 1:			$64,436		8	$134.46	
11				+++++++++		9	$135.54	
12	Value Pot 2 Needed:			*$35,564*		10	$136.62	
13	Pot 2 Value Will Be:			*$35,605* High Enough		11	$137.72	
14				+++++++++		12	$138.82	next yr.
15	Cells D12, D13 should match						--------------	
16	(Vary Cell D6 until they almost match)					108	$298.30	final mo.

Put in the 5 inputs you know, and then make a guess at *g* in cell D6. Then compare the numbers in cells D12 and D13. Cell D12 is calculated as the amount of money (Pot 2) that your future DCA investments must accrue to in the time remaining. Cell D13 gives the expected value based on your inputs and *g*. Keep trying *g* values—when they almost match *and* the cell says "High Enough" instead of "Too Low," then you have solved the problem. The columns to the right then give the investment schedule for the next 12 months as well as the investment that will be required in the final month if you stay with this plan. You could also vary any of the other inputs that seem appropriate. Here are the formulas needed to construct the spreadsheet shown above:

Formulas for Lotus 1-2-3 DCA Readjustment Program

A3:	'Final Investment Goal:
A4:	'Value of Current Holdings:
A5:	'Exp. Return Investment (*r*):
A6:	'Increase in DCA Amount (*g*):
A7:	'Amount of Last Investment:
A8:	'# Months Remaining:
A10:	'Expected Value of Pot 1:
A12:	'Value of Pot 2 Needed:
A13:	'Pot 2 Value Will Be:
C15:	'Cells D12, D13 should match
D1:	'6 INPUTS:
D3:	(C0) 100000
D4:	(C0) 22000
D5:	(P2) 0.01
D6:	(P2) 0.008
D7:	(C2) 126.16
D8:	108
D10:	(C0) +D4*(1+D5) ^ D8
D12:	(C0) +D3-D10
D13:	(C0) +D7*((1+D5) ^ D8-(1+D6) ^ D8)/(D5-D6)

E6:   ' <---
E13:   @IF(D13<D12,"Too Low","HighEnough")

F1:   ' AMOUNT TO INVEST
F2:   'in #months
F3-F14: 1 through 12
F16:   +D8

G2:   '$C
G3:   (C2) +D7*(1+D6)
G4:   (C2) +G3*(1+$D$6)
G5:   (C2) +G4*(1+$D$6)
G6:   (C2) +G5*(1+$D$6)
G7:   (C2) +G6*(1+$D$6)
G8:   (C2) +G7*(1+$D$6)
G9:   (C2) +G8*(1+$D$6)
G10:   (C2) +G9*(1+$D$6)
G11:   (C2) +G10*(1+$D$6)
G12:   (C2) +G11*(1+$D$6)
G13:   (C2) +G12*(1+$D$6)
G14:   (C2) +G13*(1+$D$6)
G16:   (C2) +D7*(1+D6)^D8

H3:   'next mo.
H14:   'next yr.
H16:   'final mo.

Establishing the Value Path 5

Chapter 4 covered plans and techniques for achieving your investment value goal with *dollar cost averaging*. Occasional readjustments to the plan were needed to eventually target in on the final investment goal. With *value averaging*, the situation is easier. By its very nature, the value averaging strategy involves a portfolio "readjustment" at every investment period, as you buy or sell shares to make your value equal the target value path.[1]

VALUE AVERAGING VALUE PATHS

There are a lot of ways to set up the *value path* for value averaging—that is, the schedule of what you want the value of your holdings to be at every point in time. Not all value paths make sense, though. Suppose you wanted to build up value monthly, resulting in $100,000 after 20 years. As presented in the "pure" linear form of value averaging, you could establish a linear value path that goes up by the same amount (1/240 of $100,000) each month. That would be an increase of $416.67 in value every month, and would require a $416.67 initial investment for the first month. As we discussed in Chapter 3, that would be an ineffective and unnatural approach that excessively front-loads the investment, while requiring no investment, or even disinvestment—later in the plan. After 19 years, the value would be $95,000. The expected monthly return on that amount (1.0%), is +$950, more than double the planned, or "allowable," increase calculated above. You would actually be expected to be a net *seller* of stock during the last 12 years of the plan.

The Value Path Formula

Value averaging requires a target value for you to achieve at each point in time. What we really need is a "compounding" value path that is similar to the value achieved with the growth-adjusted dollar cost averaging strategies. That is, we want our value averaging plan to account for: growth from expected return on our portfolio value, from monthly investment contributions, and from growth in these monthly investments. Formula **(15)** from Chapter 4 accomplishes all those things and is repeated here as formula **(19)**:

$$V_t = C \times t \times (1+R)^t \quad where \quad R = \frac{r+g}{2} \qquad (19)$$

Using this simple formula for your value path, you can construct a complete schedule of target values for every period in your investment time frame. This would take only a few quick steps with a spreadsheet. You can relate this value path to your investment goals and capabilities by setting your final value goal (such as the $V_{240} = \$100,000$ used earlier), your desired initial or average net investment contribution ($\$C$), and how much you are willing to increase your net investment contribution over time (g). Even though you will not have a consistent monthly investment amount with value averaging, you still want to set the plan up so that after accounting for an investment return on your existing shares, you still expect to put in some investment contribution (like $\$C$) to meet your value path. Depending on the market's actual performance, you will end up investing more or less than that each month—but if the market performs roughly as expected, then you should be able to handle the average net amount that you need to invest, just as with dollar cost averaging.

For example, suppose you wanted to build a fund worth $100,000 over 20 years, were willing to increase your average monthly investment contribution by 0.5% per month, and expected a 1.0% monthly return on your investment. Averaging *r* and *g*, you get $R = 0.75\%$, or 0.0075. Putting all those figures into formula **(19)**, solve for $C = \$69.34$, just as you did with dollar cost averaging. Therefore:

$$\$100,000 = \$C \times 240 \times (1.0075)^{240} = 1,442.2 \times \$C$$

$$\$C = \$69.34$$

Putting this value into the equation for *C*, this gives the target value for each month *t* from month 1 to month 240:

Sample Value Path Formula

$$V_t = \mathbf{69.34} \times t \times (1.0075)^t \tag{20}$$

This is the *growth-adjusted value path* formula. Putting in some representative values for *t*, sample points on the value path are as follows:

Month	1	$69.86	Month	60	$6,513.86
Month	2	140.77	Month	120	20,397.25
Month	3	212.74	Month	180	47,903.39
Month	12	910.13	Month	240	100,001.90
Month	24	1,991.02			

These are the target values you strive to match each month by buying or perhaps selling shares. At this rate, you make steady progress toward your final goal while smoothing out your investment exposure over time.

Flexible Variations on the Value Path Formula

What if you are *not* starting from scratch? Some investors may wish to start value averaging with existing shares that already have value. In that case, the best and most flexible method is probably for you to use a computer spreadsheet, as discussed later in this chapter. But if you are willing to calculate another formula, you can set up a value path that accounts for your investment progress to date, instead of starting from scratch. What you will do is set up a value path that is "in progress," and still has the proper length of time remaining before achieving your goal.

For example, suppose you have 17 years to develop a portfolio of $100,000, and you are happy with the $r = 1.0\%$ and $g = 0.5\%$ market return and investment growth parameters established in earlier examples. But you also have $6,500 in a fund that you want to bring into the value averaging plan as seed money. We can now figure out a value path that includes: those growth factors; has a value of $6,500 *somewhere* in the middle; and then, 17 years (204 months) later, has a value of $100,000. You see, by bringing seed money into the program, you effectively put yourself many months away from impoverished month zero. In this case, it works out that you are already effectively *87 months* into a 291-month VA strategy that ends in a value of $100,000. The difference between month 87 and month 291 is 204 months, or 17 years, which is the time you have remaining to achieve your goal. The artificial 87 months that came before your starting point are nothing more than a convenient placeholder, in that your accumulated $6,500 corresponds to what you would have now had you started from scratch 87 months ago. You simply "skipped" those 87 months by bringing that amount ($6,500) with you to the starting point.

Now we'll construct the formula you can use to begin value averaging with a head start. We'll let n be the number of periods you have available from the present in which to achieve your investment goal ($n = 204$ here). The variable t (an unknown) will designate the period number in the value path formula that corresponds to *today* (where we will have $6,500). The variable T, which we must solve for, designates the period number at the end of the value path formula (where we will have $100,000). Of course, we need to find a t (now) and a T

(later) that are n periods apart: $t = T - n$. Two variables for value, current and future, are required and should be known: v_t is our current value (\$6,500), and V_T is our required future value (\$100,000). The factor R remains an average of r and g. You can solve for T, the ending period number to use in establishing your value path, using this formula:

Head-Start VA Readjustment Formula to calculate T

$$T = \frac{n}{1 - \frac{v_t}{V_T} \times (1+R)^n} \qquad (21)$$

The derivation is shown in endnotes.[2] Solving this formula for the T that applies in this example involves putting in $v_t = 6,500$ and $V_T = 100,000$; $n = 204$ months; and $R = 0.0075$ monthly. The solution is 290.8, which we round up[3] to 291; the current time parameter t must be 87, since there must be 17 years (204 months) in between: $t = T - n = 291 - 204 = 87$. This means that instead of starting at $t = 0$ (with no initial value) and finishing at $T = 204$, we are artificially indexing the current month as $t = 87$ so as to account for the "past history" of our \$6,500 initial value. This allows for the value path formula showing a required value of \$6,500 (which we have now) at month 87 (which we will thus call *now*). Using $T = 291$ and equation **(19)**, we can solve for the specific value path formula that applies in this example by solving for \$C (as shown earlier). By placing $V_T = 100,000$ and $R = 0.0075$ along with $T = 291$ in the formula, we can calculate that $C = \$39.07$. The specific value path formula for us to follow, then, is:

$$V_t = 39.07 \times t \times (1.0075)^t \quad where \quad t = 87 \ now \qquad (22)$$

Using $t = 87$ (today's period number) in that formula gives us $V_{now} = \$6,511$, pretty close to the \$6,500 we really have. We'll set next month's target at $V_t = \$6,636$ using $t = 88$. In 17 years, when $t = 291$, our target value will be \$100,000—go ahead and plug in the number $t = 291$ and check.

NOTE: If you calculate T to be *negative*, it simply means that your final target, V_T, is too small for your head-start current value of v_t. That is, at rate R, your current investment value will grow (with no help from you) to *more* than your target value. In such a case, either reduce R, increase your final target V_T, or both, and try the calculation again.

Readjusting the VA Plan

The beauty of this addition to your bag of tools is that it allows you to *readjust* your plan and your value path to account for unforeseen changes. Suppose, for instance, you are at month 24 in the value averaging example at the beginning of this chapter, having accumulated a value of \$1,991.02 with a 20-year goal of \$100,000 (see equation **(20)**). What happens if your investment goal then changes to \$120,000, or if much higher government bond rates cause you to revise your expectation of stock market returns upward (increasing R)? You can't just start over at $t = 0$ of a new value path, nor can you ignore the nearly \$2,000 you've already accumulated. You can, however, simply use the process accompanying equation **(21)** above to put yourself "in progress" with a new value path[4] that will get you from $v_t = \$1,991.02$ now to $V_T = V_{t + 216} = \$120,000$ over the next 216 months, the remaining 18 years. (This problem is solved in endnote 4). This same situation works if your investment time frame changes or if you must take existing capital out of your investment plan to meet some unforeseen expense. The process described here gives you total flexibility in readjusting your value averaging accumulation plan for whatever changes may occur over time. And this readjustment process appears to be easier than the two-pot reverse solution method required in similar DCA cases. See the Appendix at the end of this chapter for ideas on how to use a spreadsheet to take the work out of using this important and effective investment management tool.

A Cautionary Note

The big problems occur with value averaging (or most other strategies) when you have a really bad market performance after you've already built up a sizable portfolio toward your goal. Investors approaching their final goal in December 1987 were certainly shocked and disappointed by the crash in October of 1987 and certainly would have missed their end-of-year December goal, which *had* been almost achieved. In some sense, the risk of bad performance hurts more as you get closer to your investment goal, because there's really no time to recoup losses.

To this end, it may make sense to be a bit conservative in your initial expectations. This will cause you to put a little more money in up front, but it will leave you with the welcome "problem" of exceeding your value goal more often than possibly *not* meeting it. There are a few ways to use the value path formula while being conservative. You could plan on less time, meeting your value goal for your child's college education a year early or so. You could set your final value goal at a pessimistically high level—if a range of expected public college costs in the year 2010 is given at $90,000 to $130,000, for example, you might pick the higher number (people seldom cry about having money left over). You can alternatively use lower figures for the parameters r or g, resulting in a higher initial investment, C, and a quicker wealth buildup in the early years.

An Alternate Method

For the computer literate, perhaps a better way to track the value path is with a spreadsheet rather than a formula. If the time indexing in formula (21) bothered you, this direct approach using a computer might appeal to you. Pick any number you want for the initial investment $C, and a starting value (which is 0 unless you have a "head start"). Pick your growth factors r and g. Then calculate the value path by applying the growth factors directly to the investment quantities that are growing. By setting the target value for month t equal to: the target value for the previous month times $(1 + r)$, plus the additional investment $C(1 + g)^t$, you can create the target value for every month as a function of the prior month.[5] By playing with the parameter C (and perhaps g), you can set up a value path that achieves a final value of the investment goal you have in mind. Note that formula (21) is *not* used with this alternative method. This method has the advantage of being totally flexible, because you can change parameters in mid-program and still calculate the value path over any remaining months.

SUMMARY

However you establish your value path, remember that you do not have to go to extremes to slavishly conform to it. Several variations of the strategies are discussed in this book so that you can tailor an approach to your needs using whatever variations and actions that make sense to you. It's your investment plan— the numbers can only be your guide.

Some tips on how to apply these techniques in real life are provided in Chapter 10. A full case-study example that deals with many of the complexities of a value averaging strategy is included in Chapter 11.

ENDNOTES

1.   Note that value averaging involves much more radical readjustments than occasional changes to $C or g that we undertook in dollar cost averaging. If we were over our "target value path" in dollar cost averaging, we stayed there and simply lowered our trajectory over the entire remainder of the investment period by reducing the level of, or the growth in, the monthly investment amount. The process of "getting back on track" was totally smoothed out over time. With value averaging, though, if we ever find ourselves above or below the target value path, we *immediately* get back on track by selling or buying the required number of shares.

2.   Using the value path formula (**19**) at the final investment period (T) gives the final value goal:

$$V_T = C \times T \times (1+R)^T \qquad (1)$$

We can write the same formula for the value at the intermediate point in time, v_t, realizing that $t = T - n$:

$$v_t = v_{T-n} = C \times (T-n) \times (1+R)^{T-n} \qquad (2)$$

Dividing the second equation by the first, we get:

$$\frac{v_t}{V_T} = \frac{C \times (T-n) \times (1+R)^{T-n}}{C \times T \times (1+R)^T} \qquad (3)$$

Canceling the C and $(1 + R)^T$ terms and multiplying through by $(1 + R)^n$, we get:

$$\frac{T-n}{T} = \frac{v_t}{V_T} \times (1+R)^n \qquad (4)$$

Solving this equation for T gives the formula in the text:

$$T = \frac{n}{1 - \frac{v_t}{V_T} \times (1+R)^n} \qquad (5)$$

3.   There's really no need to round it at all, but most people prefer to work with integers.

4.   For anyone playing along at home, the readjustment due to the goal increase from $100,000 to $120,000 at the 24-month point is given here. The new time parameters would be $T = 236$ and $t = 20$, and the new value path formula would be:

$$V_t = 87.18 \times t \times (1.0075)^t$$

where t is currently 20. Next month, which is now month 21, our value path goal is $2,142. We will now have to "grow" our funds more quickly to get from $1,991.02 now to $120,000 in 18 years.

5.   That is, the alternate formula for the value path for each time period t is:

$$V_t = (1+r) \times V_{t-1} + (1+g)^t \times C$$

Appendix to Chapter 5

Constructing a VA Readjustment Spreadsheet

The following spreadsheet shows the solution to the value averaging readjustment problem from Chapter 5, page 90. Start with $6,500, with 17 years (204 months) to attain a $100,000 goal, and add other inputs as shown. *What would the value path look like for monthly value averaging?*

Put in the 5 inputs you know, and the spreadsheet does all the rest. The outputs are calculated in cells B9–B12, with the value path formula in cell B14. The solution involves an artificial time index as described in the text. This is shown at the bottom of the spreadsheet, where each month is indexed by the solution $t = 86.8$. The value path is shown for current and selected future months; your spreadsheet could show the value path for all months. The spreadsheet and the formulas needed to construct the spreadsheet are shown on pages 98 and 99.

Of course, if you start with a "Value Now" of $0, this spreadsheet will calculate a standard value averaging value path, as discussed on pages 88-89.

Lotus 1-2-3 Spreadsheet, VA Readjustment Program

CELL	A	B	C
1		YOUR INPUTS	
2	Investment Goal	$100,000	
3	Value Now	$6,500	
4	Periods to Go—*n*	204	
5	*r*	1.00%	
6	*g*	0.50%	
7			
8		OUTPUTS	
9	*R*	0.75%	
10	Final Period#—*T*	290.8	
11	Time Index Now—*t*	86.8	
12	$*C*	$39.15	
13			
14	Value Path (*t*) =	39.15 x *t* x (1.0075)^*t*	
15			
16	Months From Now	Index #	Value Path
17	0	86.8	$6,500
18	1	87.8	$6,624
19	2	88.8	$6,750
20	3	89.8	$6,877
21	4	90.8	$7,006
22	.		
23	12	98.8	$8,093
24	24	110.8	$9,927
25	36	122.8	$12,034
26	.		
27	.		
28	203	289.8	$98,914
29	204	290.8	$100,000

Formulas for Lotus 1-2-3 VA Readjustment Program

```
A2:   W18] "Investment Goal
A3:   "Value Now
A4:   "Periods to Go—n
A5:   "r
A6:   "g
A9:   "R
A10:  "Final Period #—T
A11:  "Time Index Now—t
A12:  "$C
A14:  'Value Path (t) =
```

A16:   Months from Now
.A17:   0
A18:   1
A19:   2
A20:   3
A21:   4
A22:   ".
A23:   12
A24:   24
A25:   36
A26:   ".
A27:   ".
A28:   203
A29:   204

B1:   "YOUR INPUTS
B2:   (C0) 100000
B3:   (C0) 6500
B4:   204
B5:   (P2) 0.01
B6:   (P2) 0.005
B8:   "OUTPUTS
B9:   (P2) @AVG(B6..B5)
B10:   (F1) +B4/(1-(1+B9) ^ B4*B3/B2)
B11:   (F1) +B10-B4
B12:   (C2) +B2/(B10*(1+B9) ^ B10)
B14:   @STRING(B12,2)&" x t x ("&@STRING(1+B9,4)&") ^ t"
B16:   "Index #
B17:   (F1) +A17+$B$11
B18:   (F1) +A18+$B$11
B19:   (F1) +A19+$B$11
B20:   (F1) +A20+$B$11
B21:   (F1) +A21+$B$11
B23:   (F1) +A23+$B$11
B24:   (F1) +A24+$B$11
B25:   (F1) +A25+$B$11
B28:   (F1) +A28+$B$11
B29:   (F1) +A29+$B$11

C16:   "Value Path
C17:   (C0) +$B$12*B17*(1+$B$9) ^ B17
C18:   (C0) +$B$12*B18*(1+$B$9) ^ B18
C19:   (C0) +$B$12*B19*(1+$B$9) ^ B19
C20:   (C0) +$B$12*B20*(1+$B$9) ^ B20
C21:   (C0) +$B$12*B21*(1+$B$9) ^ B21
C23:   (C0) +$B$12*B23*(1+$B$9) ^ B23
C24:   (C0) +$B$12*B24*(1+$B$9) ^ B24
C25:   (C0) +$B$12*B25*(1+$B$9) ^ B25
C28:   (C0) +$B$12*B28*(1+$B$9) ^ B28
C29:   (C0) +$B$12*B29*(1+$B$9) ^ B29

Avoiding Taxes and Transaction Costs   6

"Rules are made to be broken."
". . . too much of a good thing . . ."
"You can't escape death and taxes."

As cliches go, these three aren't bad ones to keep in mind when investing. When using formula plans for "timing" investments, the very rules that can help you corral a higher return can also saddle you with unnecessary taxes and hogtie you with transaction costs. Excessive trading is expensive in terms of both commission expenses and your valuable time. Simply selling a few shares of a stock or fund may incur a tax liability, not to mention the paperwork needed for you to exercise the "privilege" of calculating and paying that tax. This chapter will analyze some of the pitfalls you may encounter in formula investing, along with some solutions that will help you tailor a plan to suit your needs.

TAX CONSIDERATIONS WITH VALUE AVERAGING

One of the advantages of value averaging and some other formula investment plans is that they help send you "sell" signals that, supposedly, enhance your investment returns. Such signals may, however, diminish your returns by causing you to pay premature taxes on your capital gains. As of 1993, there are no "tax preferences" on capital gains[1] to ease the tax burden on your profits.

The Advantage of Deferred Gains

You pay taxes on capital gains only when you *realize* the gains (sell profitable positions). Delaying the taxes on capital gains by not selling profitable shares now is beneficial on at least three counts. First, you are effectively untaxed on capital gains not yet realized upon your death. This "death loophole" is very important because the tax on capital gains would be 0% instead of 28%. For example, if you pass away holding 1,000 shares of AT&T with a profit of $7 per share, neither you, your estate, nor your heirs would be liable for a gains tax on the $7,000 profit.[2] Second, the capital gains rate may be lower in the future than it is currently. But although it is likely that some type of capital gains preference eventually pushes tax rates on gains below 28%,[3] it is always possible that they may actually *increase* instead. Finally, even if you have to pay the same tax rate on your gains in the future, it is still better to *delay* paying that tax. For example, suppose you're in the 28% tax bracket and had $10,000 invested for 10 years in an investment that steadily rose in value at 12% annually. If you paid taxes on your capital gains each year as you made them (through excessive turnover, perhaps), you would earn an after-tax annual return of only *8.64%*,[4] resulting in a final value of *$22,903*. If instead you kept all your gains *unrealized* during the 10 years, no gains taxes would be paid from year to year. In this case, your investment would rise at a pretax 12% rate to $31,058. You could then sell it, pay your 28% taxes on the profit, and keep *$25,162*. That's like earning money year by year at a *9.67%* after-tax return (compared with 8.64% above); this increased return on investment is the result of deferring the payment of taxes. Alternatively, this tax-deferred accumulation at 12% could be viewed as paying an effective tax rate, year by year, of only 19.4% (as opposed to 28% above).[5] Either way you look at it, you're cutting yourself a break if you delay taxes by keeping capital gains *in* your portfolio.

Deferring Capital Gains Taxes: An Example

We'll use the mutual fund example (from Chapters 2 and 3) of the value averaging strategy to analyze the tax disadvantage that comes with share selling. That example covered two years, but we want to look at a longer period because several years must pass before there's any noticeable difference as a consequence of tax deferral; that is, the difference between the cost of paying taxes now (as we sell shares with VA) and the cost of paying taxes later (by never selling, as with DCA). In either case, taxes will take a serious bite out of investment return. The goal is to get a sense of *how much more* return we give up to taxes by selling earlier with value averaging. Conversely, we want to know *how big* the tax-deferral advantage is as a consequence of *keeping* all shares with dollar cost averaging.

Additional data were collected for 25 more months on this mutual fund, giving us 50 months of data. Although not presented in tabular form in prior chapters due to the bulk of numbers, the results of this extended 4-year analysis were mentioned in Chapter 3: rates of return were 3.9% for CS, 6.8% for DCA, and 13.8% for the VA strategy. These returns were all *pretax* and are the actual returns I would have received only if the fund holdings were part of an IRA or other tax-sheltered program.[6] The monthly prices over this four-year period are shown in the columns 1–2 of Table 6-1, which shows the tax effects of pursuing a value averaging strategy over this period with the fund. Our goal is to take *all* the cash flows, including any *taxes*, and calculate the true *after-tax* rate of return from the strategy. After doing this in Table 6-1, we can then compare the after-tax rate of return from value averaging to that from dollar cost averaging. Because no shares are sold with the DCA strategy, all capital gains taxes are deferred to the end of the investment period; thus, month-by-month cash flows for DCA are not shown separately.

There are four pairs of columns in Table 6-1: columns 1–2 give the month (Mo #1 = January 1986) and the share price; columns 3-4 implement a $100-a-month pure value averaging strategy; columns 5–6 establish the share cost basis for tax purposes for all mutual fund shares held; and the final columns calculate the tax paid on profits from sales. You need

TABLE 6-1 After-Tax Rate of Return when Value Averaging Profits Are Taxable							
Mutual Fund		Value Averaging		Share Cost Basis		Tax Info	
Mo	Share Price	Shares Owned	($$$) Invested	Total Basis	Basis per Share	Realized Profit	Tax @ 28%
1	$4.64	21.55	($100.00)	$100.0	$4.64	$0.00	$0.00
2	$4.38	45.66	($105.60)	205.6	$4.50	$0.00	$0.00
3	$4.56	65.79	($91.78)	297.4	$4.52	$0.00	$0.00
4	$4.25	94.12	($120.39)	417.8	$4.44	$0.00	$0.00
5	$3.81	131.23	($141.41)	559.2	$4.26	$0.00	$0.00
6	$3.19	188.09	($181.36)	740.6	$3.94	$0.00	$0.00
7	$2.99	234.11	($137.62)	878.2	$3.75	$0.00	$0.00
8	$3.60	222.22	$42.81	833.6	$3.75	($1.80)	$0.00
9	$4.70	191.49	$144.44	718.3	$3.75	$29.16	$7.66
10	$4.41	226.76	($155.53)	873.8	$3.85	$0.00	$0.00
11	$4.34	253.46	($115.87)	989.7	$3.90	$0.00	$0.00
12	$4.69	255.86	($11.29)	1001.0	$3.91	$0.00	$0.00
13	$5.26	247.15	$45.84	966.9	$3.91	$11.75	$3.29
14	$4.54	308.37	($277.95)	1244.9	$4.04	$0.00	$0.00
15	$5.38	278.81	$159.03	1125.5	$4.04	$39.70	$11.12
16	$7.47	214.19	$482.71	864.6	$4.04	$221.85	$62.12
17	$7.39	230.04	($117.14)	981.8	$4.27	$0.00	$0.00
18	$6.31	285.26	($348.44)	1330.2	$4.66	$0.00	$0.00
19	$7.07	268.74	$116.80	1253.2	$4.66	$39.76	$11.13
20	$6.48	308.64	($258.56)	1511.7	$4.90	$0.00	$0.00
21	$7.07	297.03	$82.10	1454.9	$4.90	$25.22	$7.06
22	$6.96	316.09	($132.67)	1587.5	$5.02	$0.00	$0.00
23	$5.05	455.45	($703.74)	2291.3	$5.03	$0.00	$0.00
24	$5.80	413.79	$241.58	2081.7	$5.03	$32.04	$8.97
25	$5.06	494.07	($406.21)	2488.0	$5.04	$0.00	$0.00
26	$4.65	559.14	($302.57)	2790.5	$4.99	$0.00	$0.00
27	$4.77	566.04	($32.90)	2823.4	$4.99	$0.00	$0.00
28	$4.42	633.48	($298.11)	3121.5	$4.93	$0.00	$0.00
29	$4.00	725.00	($366.06)	3487.6	$4.81	$0.00	$0.00
30	$4.20	714.29	$45.00	3436.0	$4.81	($6.54)	$0.00
31	$3.95	784.81	($278.57)	3714.6	$4.73	$0.00	$0.00

TABLE 6-1 After-Tax Rate of Return when Value Averaging Profits Are Taxable, *Cont'd*							
Mutual Fund		Value Averaging		Share Cost Basis		Tax Info	
Mo	Share Price	Shares Owned	($$$) Invested	Total Basis	Basis per Share	Realized Profit	Tax @ 28%
32	$3.50	914.29	($453.16)	4168	$4.56	$0.00	$0.00
33	$3.18	1037.74	($392.57)	4560	$4.39	$0.00	$0.00
34	$3.41	997.07	$138.68	4382	$4.39	($40.04)	$0.00
35	$3.65	958.90	$139.30	4214	$4.39	($28.41)	$0.00
36	$3.41	1055.72	($330.14)	4544	$4.30	$0.00	$0.00
37	$3.32	1114.46	($195.01)	4739	$4.25	$0.00	$0.00
38	$3.33	1141.14	($88.86)	4828	$4.23	$0.00	$0.00
39	$3.93	992.37	$584.68	4198	$4.23	($44.75)	$0.00
40	$3.85	1038.96	($179.39)	4378	$4.21	$0.00	$0.00
41	$3.58	1145.25	($380.52)	4758	$4.15	$0.00	$0.00
42	$3.51	1196.58	($180.17)	4939	$4.13	$0.00	$0.00
43	$3.90	1102.56	$366.67	4551	$4.13	($21.36)	$0.00
44	$3.94	1116.75	($55.90)	4606	$4.12	$0.00	$0.00
45	$3.97	1133.50	($66.50)	4673	$4.12	$0.00	$0.00
46	$3.76	1223.40	($338.04)	5011	$4.10	$0.00	$0.00
47	$4.81	977.13	$1184.57	4002	$4.10	$175.86	$9.73
48	$5.47	877.51	$544.91	3594	$4.10	$136.88	$38.33
49	$6.10	803.28	$452.83	3290	$4.10	$148.77	$41.66
50	$5.01	0.00	$4024.43	*sold all shares*		$734.26	$205.59

Summary of Rates of Return for DCA and VA Strategies (Annualized)

Strategy	Before-Tax IRR	After-Tax IRR	Effective Tax Rate[7]
Value Averaging	13.8%	9.9%	27.0%
Dollar Cost Averaging	6.8%	5.0%	26.3%

the cost basis of your shares to know how much profit you've made so you can pay gains taxes on it. The average cost method is used to establish the cost basis—you simply keep a running average of the cost of any purchased shares.[8] Tax is calculated for any sales of shares by figuring out the profit (e.g., the amount of money received minus the cost basis of the shares sold). Look at month 8, where the big rise in share price to $3.60 caused a sale of 11.89 shares for a total $42.81 received. The average cost basis of each share was $3.75 by then (or $44.61 for all shares sold), so for accounting purposes there is a loss of ($1.80), carried over until a profit occurs to offset it.[9] This happens in the next month, when a huge rise in price to $4.70 results in a sale of $144.44 worth of the fund, and a profit of $29.16. The tax on the $29.16 is simply 28% of that profit, or $8.16. In this case, though, we still had $1.80 of accrued losses from the month before, so the tax bill, net for both months, is $7.66. Our before-tax cash flow of +$144.44 for month 9 is reduced by this tax paid, resulting in a net after-tax cash flow of +$136.78 (not shown, but this quantity is used to calculate the after-tax IRR).

This process is repeated through month 49, when the value path stops at $4,900. Then after the following (and final) month, after a huge price decline, the entire remaining portfolio is revalued at the final price of $5.01, and taxes are paid on the $734.26 profit from that final sale. Now we can look at all the net-of-tax cash flows from value averaging and calculate the after-tax rate of return on those flows. This is done in the bottom portion of the table. In this example, the after-tax annualized IRR, using value averaging, was 9.9% compared with a pretax IRR of 13.8%. This 9.9% return is equivalent to having paid a tax rate of 27.0%, smoothed out over the entire period.[10] That is, there's only a small reduction in effective taxes (below 28%) due to tax deferral, because only a portion (the final $734.26) of the profit was tax-deferred; the rest, due to early sales, was pay-as-you-go.

We can now compare these results to DCA results. Recall that the before-tax return from DCA in this example was only 6.8%, less than half of the VA return. But because dollar cost averaging does not result in the "premature" payment of taxes due to selling, its tax-deferral advantage should help it close this gap. We don't need a table for the dollar cost averaging analysis, because there is only one tax payment, in month 50, when we terminate both strategies. Deducting this final 28% tax payment from the sales proceeds in month 50, the series of net-of-tax dollar cost averaging cash flows yield an after-tax rate of return of 5.0%. This is equivalent to having had no tax deferral, but instead having paid the tax on profits smoothed over the period at an effective 26.3% tax rate.

There was a 1.7% "tax rate reduction" (28% - 26.3% = 1.7%) due to full deferral with the dollar cost averaging strategy; there was a 1.0% tax rate reduction with value averaging. In terms of return, the 0.7% higher effective tax rate of value averaging only hurts the annualized return to the tune of -0.07%.[11] That simply pales in comparison to the +4.90% difference between the actual after-tax returns of 5.0% (DCA) and 9.9% (VA).

In concluding this analysis, it is important to distinguish between the general *conceptual* advantage to tax deferral and the rather small cost (incurred by selling shares) of giving up some of this deferral advantage by using value averaging. The tax cost of the sales in value averaging can be small, perhaps even insignificant, over short- and medium-term investment periods. Furthermore, should tax rates increase in the future, even this small cost could disappear altogether.

A Compromise: No-Sell Value Averaging

There is, of course, a simple alternative to selling shares as dictated by value averaging, and that is to simply *not* sell them. The *no-sell* variation of value averaging is explained as follows: If the value of your holdings exceeds your value goal for the period, simply do nothing. Suppose, for example, your value goal was increasing by $100 a month, and after a year you had a fund worth $1,200. Next month, the fund value increases 10% to $1,320, thus exceeding by $20 your new value goal of $1,300. Don't sell the $20 worth of "extra value" shares; just hang on to the whole $1,320 fund until next month. Then a month later, if the share price remains steady, you would have to invest $80 to make your $1,320 holdings increase to the new value goal of $1,400. This way, if you get ahead of the game by exceeding your value goal, you can "slow down" and invest nothing until the increasing value goal eventually catches up with your portfolio value. This not only eliminates taxes or transaction costs associated with selling; it also smooths out the buying and saves you time and energy.

By forgoing selling, you are really affecting only one-half of the distinctive character of a value averaging strategy. You'll still be buying more shares when the share price has fallen; you just won't be selling shares when it rises. But by not investing anything after large market increases (as opposed to, say, investing $100 with DCA), you'll still be making a relative move away from the market, as compared to dollar cost averaging. The move just won't be as drastic as with a pure value averaging strategy, where you would actually sell shares.

Theoretically, the cost of pursuing the no-sell variation should be in the form of lower returns, because no-sell value averaging is a sort of middle ground between dollar cost averaging and value averaging. Thus, we'd expect the investment returns to be somewhere between those two pure strategies. We'll now look at two examples to get a feel for how much of value averaging's incremental return is "given back" if you decide not to sell when indicated.

First, take a look at the mutual fund example from earlier in this chapter. Table 6-2 shows what happens if you apply the no-sell variation of value averaging over the same period. Up through month 7, Table 6-2 looks much like the first four columns of Table 6-1, but the last column of Table 6-2 shows no action taken where in Table 6-1 sales had been indi-

TABLE 6-2 Rate of Return when *No-Sell* Value Averaging Is Used					
Mutual Fund		Value Averaging			
Mo	Share Price	Shares Owned	Actual Value	Value Goal	($$$) Invested
1	$4.64	21.55	$100.00	$100.00	($100.00)
2	$4.38	45.66	200.00	$200.00	($105.60)
3	$4.56	65.79	300.00	$300.00	($91.78)
4	$4.25	94.12	400.00	$400.00	($120.39)
5	$3.81	131.23	500.00	$500.00	($141.41)
6	$3.19	188.09	600.00	$600.00	($181.36)
7	$2.99	234.11	700.00	$700.00	($137.62)
8	$3.60	234.11	**842.80**	**$800.00**	$0.00
9	$4.70	234.11	**1,100.32**	**$900.00**	$0.00
10	$4.41	234.11	**1,032.43**	**$1,000.00**	$0.00
11	$4.34	253.46	1,100.00	$1,100.00	($83.95)
12	$4.69	255.86	1,200.00	$1,200.00	($11.29)
13	$5.26	255.86	**1,345.82**	**$1,300.00**	$0.00
14	$4.54	308.37	1,400.00	$1,400.00	($238.38)
.	.	.	.	.	.
.	.	.	.	.	.
.	.	.	.	.	.
.	.	.	.	.	.
49	$6.10	1223.40	**7,462.74**	**$4,900.00**	$0.00
50	$5.01	0.00		*sold all shares*	*$6,129.23*

Taxes of $347.79 paid on $1,242.11 capital gain

Summary of Rates of Return

Strategy	Before-Tax IRR	After-Tax IRR
Value Avg	13.8%	9.9%
No-Sell VA	10.9%	8.0%
DC Avg	6.8%	5.0%

cated. Thus, you can have an actual value that exceeds your value goal. In months 8 and 9, the share price increased far more than the value path, so no purchase or sale was made. In month 10, the fund price went down, but the $1,032 portfolio value still exceeded the $1,000 value goal; again, no action taken. Note that in these three months the value of the portfolio exceeds the value goal. In month 11, the portfolio value *finally* falls below the value goal, so shares are again purchased. But note that we see fewer shares purchased that month in Table 6-2 (no-sell VA) than in Table 6-1 (pure VA), because the "excess" from the preceding month accrued to replace some of the required share purchase. Jumping down to month 49, we see it was just like month 8 in that no action was required due to a big price increase in month 49 (and in fact, in the prior two months as well). Finally, the portfolio value at month 50 is $6,129.23, providing a taxable profit of $1,242.11 and leaving cash proceeds of $5,781.44 after paying the 28% taxes.

The effect of not selling in this value averaging implementation is shown at the bottom of the table. The pretax rate of return from this variation is 10.9%, a bit closer to the 13.8% return of "pure" VA than to the lower 6.8% DCA return. The after-tax IRRs line up the same way. The small tax savings from not using "normal" selling is far more than offset by the return diminution from not using "normal" value averaging, in this example.

The second example of no-sell value averaging effectiveness uses all the data on monthly stock returns from Chapter 1. The figures in Table 6-3 are the same as those in Table 3-3c, except for the addition of the no-sell value averaging strategy. The (pretax) annualized rate of return is given for monthly investing over the entire 66-year period, growth equalized as discussed in previous chapters. The results show that although the actual long-run effect of not selling has not affected the return on a value averaging strategy by much, there is still some cost to it. Such a strategy never would have allowed for selling

TABLE 6-3 Comparison of Strategies: 1926–1991 DCA, No-Sell VA, and VA, "Growth-Equalized"			
Strategy:	DCA	No-Sell VA	VA
Rate of Return:	11.46%	12.32%	12.56%

shares during the 1987 pre-Crash extreme run-up in prices. Furthermore, it would not have allowed for purchasing shares during the three major market dips after 1975. Implementing such a strategy would have to take into account the possibility of your value path never catching up with your portfolio value for a decade at a time. This and other complications will be discussed in later chapters.

REDUCING TRANSACTION COSTS

There is no doubt that transaction costs (including taxes) can play a major role in keeping investors from achieving their goals—a fact that should be kept in mind when using a formula plan. Structure your plan so that unnecessary transaction costs can be minimized or, if possible, avoided altogether. This section includes several ideas about how to set up a reasonably economical version of value averaging.

Limiting Taxes

Besides the no-sell version of value averaging just covered, there are a few less extreme ways of limiting your capital gains taxes without accepting lower returns. The first is to delay or limit selling. A one-period delay in selling will reduce your returns a little, but not nearly as much as the no-sell version. As will be seen in a later chapter on market overreaction, there actually may be good theoretical reasons for you to wait one month before selling, once selling is indicated. Placing a limit on selling is a reasonable hybrid strategy, and it avoids wild moves in your portfolio while potentially reducing taxes.

A second approach has to do with the way capital gains taxes are actually paid. You don't pay taxes on any gains incurred during the year until next April. So if in the last few months of the year profitable selling is dictated by your value averaging strategy, it may make good sense to delay the sale until early the next year (if a sale is still needed then). That way the taxes on the gains won't be due until a year later. In the same vein, because you pay taxes only on your *net* capital gains, so you can use capital losses to offset capital gains. If you have accumulated some net capital losses (don't do this on purpose!) and your value averaging strategy later that same year calls for some profitable sales, your losses will shelter some or all of your gains. Due to the time value of money, "using" your existing capital losses this year is worth more than carrying them over to later years.

Limiting Costs

There are a few things you can do to limit other transaction costs in your investment plan. Most of it is just common sense, but it probably bears mentioning anyway.

The best thing you can do with any plan that will incur taxes in its execution is simply to put those assets in a tax-advantaged account. If you plan to use value averaging, it would make sense to do it under the umbrella of an IRA, Keogh, or other tax-sheltered plan. If you did this, you would need some type of "side fund" (such as a money market fund) under the same umbrella, because you don't have full freedom to move in and out of such tax-sheltered accounts.

A sensible way to reduce transaction costs—and increase diversification (to reduce risk) as well—is to use no-load mutual funds. Although this book is not a treatise on mutual funds, it should be mentioned that index funds are a particularly good choice in that they mirror the market closely and have extremely low management fees and expense ratios. In any case, stay away from loads and fees that will hamstring your performance in a strategy where occasionally you may want to sell fund shares.

A few other things you could do to reduce transaction costs, particularly your time and energy, are simple and reasonable variations that make the strategy more practical. For example, you could "revalue" your portfolio less often; that is, take action less frequently to meet your value goal. We have been using a monthly investment. As you will see in Chapter 9 on market overreaction, it is probably better (and has proven better in the past) to "do" value averaging quarterly instead of monthly. Another sensible and minor variation is simply to refrain from very small trades or to round your required purchase off to the nearest $100 or so. This way you wouldn't need to invest or sell as often and you'd save on time, transaction costs, and tax liability.

SUMMARY

This chapter explored ways to keep taxes and transaction costs from interfering too much with the success of your investment strategy. We've seen that taxes should not be your primary consideration when designing your own value averaging plan, because the tax savings from a no-sell variation of the plan are far exceeded by a reduction in return, even for reasonably long periods of time. Several alternative VA variations work quite well, so that transaction costs in a tailored strategy can be kept under control.

It is hoped that this information will help you decide just how far to go to reduce taxes and other costs and set up a plan with reasonable expenses you can live with. Other practical guidelines to help you take advantage of value averaging to best suit your investment needs will be discussed in Chapters 10 and 11.

ENDNOTES

1.   As of this writing, though, there is a cap of 28% on certain long-term capital gains that provides an indirect capital gains preference for taxpayers in the upper bracket.

2.   Of course, *estate* tax provisions still apply, but this is a separate matter from *income* taxes.

3.   Due to complicated deduction phase-outs and other complex interactions in the tax code, the 28% rate "cap" can effectively be exceeded in some circumstances.

4.   In the 28% bracket, you get to keep 72% of your marginal income; 72% of 12% is 8.64%, your after-tax rate of return.

5.   If you earned 12% and paid 19.4% tax on gains each year, you would get to keep 80.6% (100% - 19.4%) of your 12% return; this is 9.67% (80.6% of 12%), the after-tax return of the tax-deferred accumulation.

6.   Of course, even these programs only *defer* the taxes until later, upon withdrawal. But there would be no immediate tax on any intermediate income or profits, allowing all of your income to compound tax free.

7.   The effective tax rate is calculated by comparing the *monthly* before-tax and after-tax rate of return on each strategy. You get a slightly higher number (for each strategy) if you use the annualized rate of return, because it is a "nonlinear transformation" of the monthly figure.

8.   For explanation of this and other basis methods, along with helpful detailed instructions for creating spreadsheets to continually calculate your basis, see: Edward L. Ostrom, Jr., "Determining the Cost Basis of Mutual Fund Shares," *Computerized Investing*, Mar/Apr 1990, pp. 10–14.

9.   This was done to be conservative in evaluating value averaging so as to avoid making the returns look good due to early "tax subsidy" of losses. Also, for much the same reason, taxes are paid monthly here instead of annually. Thus, the return-reduction due to taxes, actually experienced by a VA investor, will generally be less adverse than that shown here.

10. Using the monthly IRRs of 1.082% pretax (which is 13.8% annualized) and 0.790% post-tax (which is 9.9% annualized), the - 0.292% difference is 27.0% of the pretax return.

11. If the 1.082% monthly pretax rate of return of value averaging had been subject to the DCA effective tax rate of 26.3% (as opposed to 27.0% for VA), the post-tax return would have been about 0.795% monthly, or 9.97% annualized. Compared to the true after-tax VA return of 9.90%, this is only a 0.07% improvement in rate of return due to deferred tax effects. Said differently, the rate of return "penalty" suffered by VA due to taxes on early sales, was only 0.07% in this case.

Playing Simulation Games 7

So far, we have used only historical market data to analyze the strengths, weaknesses, and returns of various formula strategies. This fact instills in many people a certain confidence, in that these strategies have worked in actual market conditions we all have lived through. But analyses using *only* historical data may give investors a false sense of security. This chapter, therefore, explains a different but complementary approach—*market simulations*[1]—for analyzing possible outcomes and typical performance of various investment strategies.

WHY SIMULATIONS?

In the past, many possible future outcomes existed for the stock market. Much like today, no one in 1926 knew what the market would do in the next year. In retrospect, we have seen what actually happened, but that was just one of an infinite number of possible market histories. Think of the return on the market as being random, like a roll of the dice.[2] If you rolled the dice yesterday and an 11 came up, would you really base your future betting strategy on that same 11 coming up again next time?

Like the roll of the dice, the market return in any given future period is uncertain. So, what's the danger in using only historical data to test various investment strategies? After all, it's reassuring to know how a particular strategy worked in the past. But under an even slightly different future scenario, the results might differ substantially. In fact, lots of ways to supposedly "beat the market" can be devised through *back-testing*, a 20/20 hindsight method of finding what worked best in the past.

Any number of plans will look good *if* the future turns out exactly like yesteryear, but we also want to know how robustly those seemingly good results would perform in a multitude of possible alternative futures.

WHAT AND HOW?

If we don't know *what* the market will do in the future, then *how* can we possibly construct a market simulation? In a nutshell, we generate random possible futures for the market that are *centered* on what we *expect* (on average in the long run) from the market and that are *spread out* in a random fashion around that center to an extent that reflects our *uncertainty* about—that is, the expected *variability* of—future market returns. More likely market outcomes will be generated more often; and, although extreme outcomes will occur, they will not be generated nearly as often as normal ones.

Parameters

The catch to this simulation procedure is getting some predetermined notion of the *center* and the *spread* we expect for the future. We need these two market *parameters* to generate simulation results that are reasonable—results that, although random, are in line with what we might reasonably expect today about tomorrow's market. The bad news is, we can't arrive at those numbers with any certainty. But the good news is that we can *estimate* them based in part on what we've seen in the past. That is, whereas we can't predict with confidence what will happen next year, we probably can make sensible observations about the long-run average performance of the market. Suppose, for example, you knew a single die was weighted to favor one number slightly, but didn't know which number. If it comes up a 5, you really can't say a whole lot about the next roll because you just don't know enough about the die yet. But if you track the die over 100 rolls and it comes up 6 twice as often as the other numbers, you now have something. You still don't know what will happen on the next roll, but you suspect a 6 is about twice as likely to come up as any other number. This scenario is just like setting up a market simulation—we don't know *exactly* what will happen (due to uncontrollable uncertainty), but we have reasonable expectations about where the outcome of the market is "weighted" from watching the many "rolls" of previous periods—e.g., historical market data.

Expected Return

The expected return on the market will be the *center* around which our random outcomes will be designed to fall. In Chapter 1, we took a look at historical returns and found that over the 66 years of data analyzed, the rate of return on the stock market was about 7% higher than the return on long-term government bonds. It may be reasonable to project this relationship into long-term expectations for the future. With long-term interest rates currently at about 7-8%, we calculated the expected return on the market currently to be about 14-15% (we'll use 15%).[3] Even though we can never know if this educated guess is correct, it is certainly a more reasonable number than 10% (which is too low—no sophisticated investor would invest in risky stocks) or 20% (I wish!). Over *good* future periods, of course, returns will be well over 15% annually; for *bad* future times, returns will be less. But if we don't have a copy of next year's newspaper, the best we can do is make a reasoned estimate of what we expect based on familiar relationships. We'll use 1.25%[4] as the center of our monthly returns in the simulation.

Expected Variability

The expected variability on the market will be the *spread* with which we design the random market outcomes to fall around the *center*. From the historical data analyzed in Chapter 1, we found that the annualized variability on market returns was slightly over 20% (the *standard deviation*), although it was less than that during the postwar era. We'll take the expected market variability to be 19% annually[5] or 5.5% monthly.[6]

   Using these reasonable estimates, we will construct a simulation that randomly picks out monthly returns that are distributed around a center of +1.25% per month with a standard deviation of 5.5%. Recall from Chapter 1 that this measure of spread gives probability measures of how wildly you can expect the random returns to vary around the expected center.[7] We can expect roughly two-thirds of the random outcomes to fall within one deviation of the center and about 95% of them to fall within two deviations. This means that about two-thirds of the monthly returns will fall between -4.25% and +6.75%. In annual terms, the "two-thirds range" is between -4% and +34% annual return.

Randomness

It is important to note that by choosing the two parameters above, we are not "forcing" each individual random outcome of the simulation to look like past market outcomes. The simulation allows for a wide range of possibilities, including many you might scoff at, since they wouldn't "look like" market price movements to you. But we have to get over this natural bias toward thinking that the map of future market movements is going to be just like some period from the past. All we are forcing with the simulation is that the *average* characteristics of a huge number of randomly generated outcomes will look something like what we expect. Of course, that means individual outcomes that are closest to our experience and expectations will occur more often than "unusual" ones. That is, you will see a lot more years in the simulation with a 15% gain than with a 40% gain. So, although the results of the simulation are random, they should make sense and seem reasonable.

CONSTRUCTING THE SIMULATION

The results of several simulations will be shown in Chapter 8 to evaluate the strategies in various situations. Discussed here are the mechanics of how to set up a simulation of monthly stock returns over a 5-year period. The random share price follows a *normal diffusion process,* that is, it is truly random, but *on average* it has an expected annual return of +15%, with a standard deviation of about 19%.

The simulation is constructed on a spreadsheet and consists of five basic steps:

1. Generate a series of normally distributed random numbers, one for each period you wish to simulate.
2. Convert the normally distributed random numbers into a series of normally distributed random monthly stock returns with an average outcome of 1.25% and a standard deviation of 5.5%.
3. Convert the stock returns into a stock price—use any index, such as 1.00, for the first month and then adjust it by each monthly return.
4. Use the series of monthly stock prices generated to evaluate whatever investment strategies you are interested in, as done with the actual mutual fund data in Chapters 2 and 3. Steps 1 through 4 constitute a single *run,* or outcome, of the simulation.
5. Repeat steps 1 through 4 many times, so that you have many runs over which to analyze the performance of your strategies.

In the next chapter, we will see many variations of formula strategies evaluated over hundreds of *runs* to get a basic feel for how they might perform over a wide range of plausible future circumstances.

Readers interested in the deeper details of creating their own simulations should make use of the Appendix at the end of this chapter.

An Example

This random simulation will be used many times in Chapter 8. An example of just one of these many runs of simulated 5-year comparisons is portrayed in Figure 7-1. This particular run actually comes surprisingly close to expected market performance. Other runs of the simulation are, on average, typical of average historical stock market returns. The "share price" is indexed to start at $10 and ends up at $20.56 in this particular simulation.[8] The graph shows both of the accumulation strategies "working their magic"—keeping the average *cost* per share purchased below the average *price* per share. Dollar cost averaging gradually reduces its cost by over $1 per share to $15.70, less than the $16.68 average price for the 60 months, by buying less of the high-priced shares. But value averaging goes even further by *selling* high-priced shares, keeping the net average cost per share ($14.27) much lower. The rate of return for value averaging is +13.5%, only +10.7% for dollar cost averaging, and 9.4% for the share-a-month CS (average price)[9] strategy.

This single run of the simulation proves nothing; it is shown only to give you an idea of what one simulation run involves. The idea is not to run the simulation once and com-

Figure 7-1 RANDOM SIMULATION RESULTS, 1–RUN

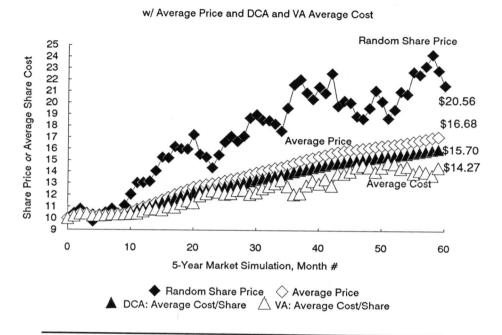

w/ Average Price and DCA and VA Average Cost

◆ Random Share Price   ◇ Average Price
▲ DCA: Average Cost/Share   △ VA: Average Cost/Share

Shows the random share price (top) from one single run of the 5-year simulation. Also shows that the net average cost per share with VA is less than that for DCA, which is less than the average share price.

pare strategies but to do it *many* times, letting the randomness "average out" to get a better sense of how the strategies perform over a wide range of feasible outcomes.

If we perform many runs of the simulation, we will get many different random price paths for our simulated "stock." In Figure 7-2, the annual compound increase in the random stock's price over the 5-year simulation period is tabulated over

Figure 7-2 DISTRIBUTION OF RANDOM STOCK RETURNS

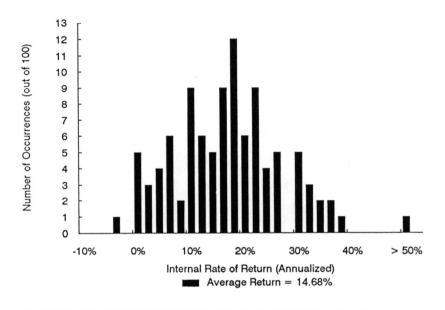

5-Year Market Simulation, 100 runs

Internal Rate of Return (Annualized)
■ Average Return = 14.68%

The random market simulation was run 100 times. Outcomes fall into a 2% range below the number shown—for instance, the 5 occurrences shown at 0% mean the annualized return fell between -2% and 0% five times.

100 runs of the simulation. The 100 random 5-year results are centered over the average annual return of 14.68%, which is pretty close to what we expected. But each individual 5-year simulation had a return that varied in a widely scattered fashion around that center. Six out of 100 times, there was a reduction in share price (negative return) over the 5-year period, but only once was it a serious drop. Once out of 100 runs, the return was staggeringly high. The results of the single simulation shown in Figure 7-1 is just one of these 100 runs shown in Figure 7-2.

Figure 7-3 DISTRIBUTION OF RANDOM STOCK RETURNS

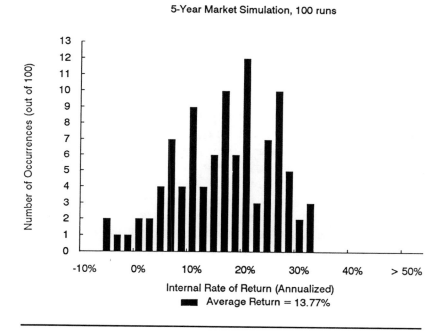

5-Year Market Simulation, 100 runs

Similar to Figure 7-2, these are the results of 100 runs of our 5-year simulated market.

Another 100 runs of the simulation will yield a different set of "future market paths." Figure 7-3 is similar to Figure 7-2, except that a second 100 simulations were run. Noting how different the two figures are should help you understand how the simulations are in fact random. The wildly positive return that occurred in Figure 7-2 did not happen any of these 100 times. Note though that the basic shape and center are pretty close. There were even six "losing" runs out of 100 in both cases.[10] Because each single run of the simulation represents five years of market data, we have covered the equivalent of 1,000 years of market data with these 200 simulation runs. In

Chapter 8, we will use many runs of the simulation to test our strategies over a wide range (as shown in Figures 7-2 and 7-3) of possible market outcomes.

ENDNOTES

1.   These are called *Monte Carlo simulations* and are a fairly common method of evaluating the properties of numerical methods (such as the rules and performance of formula strategies).

2.   Actually, it's not so much the *market* that is random, but the *information surprises* that arrive in a random fashion. Information (such as unexpected drops in interest rates, low corporate profits, oil price shocks, world tensions, etc.) drives market returns, sometimes steering unpredictably. As long as some portion of market-related information develops in an unpredictable manner, the resulting stock returns will appear unpredictable and random.

3.   Actually, 13-14% may be a better estimate than 14-15%. The reason is a bit complex, but here it is in a nutshell. Market volatility today is not quite as high as in the 66 years of data we've examined. If the additional return of stocks over bonds is a function of risk, then the stock risk premium is probably closer to 6% than to 7%. Luckily, using one estimate instead of the other makes little difference in analyzing the various investment strategies.

4.   The figure 1.25% equals 15% divided by 12 months. For reasons involving a tool called *stochastic calculus* that are too detailed to get into, you can't use the "de-annualized" monthly return of 1.1715%, because it would cause the annual returns from the simulation to fall below the 15% we expect. In rough terms, this has to do with the randomness, and the effect of a -10% return (from which you need a +11.1% return to recover) being "bigger" than a +10% return.

5.   There is a way to use index *options* prices to infer the currently expected variability on the market. These methods are well beyond the scope of this book, but the results lead us to believe that historical variability (over 20%) is a bit higher than what we typically expect today, mainly due to excessively wild movement during the Great Depression.

6. Statistically we expect that the variability (as measured by the standard deviation) of random returns over time is related by the square root of the relative time. In this case, because a month is 1/12 of a year, we expect the standard deviation of monthly returns to be only SQRT(1/12), or 0.29, times the annual deviation (19%); this is 5.5%.

7. This assumes a particular bell curve-shaped distribution of the random outcomes, called the *normal distribution*. This has been found by Professor Eugene Fama (of the University of Chicago) and others to be a reasonable description of the way monthly stock prices are actually distributed in real life. Using another theoretical possibility called the *log-normal distribution* is also reasonable. I did this, but the simulation results changed only a little bit, and in the direction of making value averaging rates of return relatively higher. The unnecessary complexity of that simulation and its parameters prohibit inclusion in this book.

8. This simulation resulted in a price increase at a roughly 15% compound annual rate. This rate would apply only to an investor buying all the "stock" up front and holding it for the entire time with no intermediate purchases. Because the intermediate price movements and cash flows that are so important in the accumulation strategies (CS, DCA, and VA) are irrelevant to the rate of return on the underlying stock itself, this rate cannot be compared with the rate on the formula strategies.

9. The constant share (CS) strategy results in an average share cost that is exactly the average price of the share over the period. This is obvious, as if you buy 1 share at each price, the average cost *is* the average price.

10. This is merely a coincidence, not a "requirement" of the simulation process.

Appendix to Chapter 7

Constructing a Simulation

Many readers have no interest in the underlying details of the simulation process. However, a multitude of readers have requested information on how to run a test of this or that strategy. Readers in this category may try to create a simulation for their own purposes. This Appendix should help.

SIMULATION STEPS

The simulation is constructed on a spreadsheet and consists of five basic steps:

1. Generate a series of normally distributed random numbers, one for each period you wish to simulate.
2. Convert the normally distributed random numbers into a series of normally distributed random monthly stock returns with an average outcome of 1.25% and a standard deviation of 5.5%.
3. Convert the stock returns into a stock price—use any index, such as 1.00, for the first month, and then adjust it by each monthly return.
4. Use the series of monthly stock prices generated to evaluate whatever investment strategies you are interested in, as done with the actual mutual fund data in Chapters 2 and 3. Steps 1 through 4 constitute a single *run*, or outcome, of the simulation.
5. Repeat steps 1 through 4 many times, so that you have many runs over which to analyze the performance of your strategies.

For someone trying this at home, the hardest steps to understand usually are steps 1 and 2, the generation of the normally distributed simulated market returns. The first part of step 1 is simply to generate 60[a] standard normal random numbers—one for each month. You will need 60 *different* random numbers for each run of a 5-year monthly simulation.

CREATING NORMALLY DISTRIBUTED
RANDOM NUMBERS
An Alternate Method

The text describes a method of converting spreadsheet (uniform) random numbers into numbers that have (approximately) a standard normal distribution. It is simple, but it is not exact, and it eats up a lot of cells on the spreadsheet. In most cases, though, it should suit your simulation needs just fine.

For more advanced spreadsheet users who can use the *"macro"* feature of spreadsheets, there is an alternative method. This method takes two spreadsheet (uniform) random numbers, and converts them into two independent numbers drawn from a normal distribution with a mean of 0 and a standard deviation of 1 (called *standard normal random numbers*). Here are the steps:

1.   Generate 2 uniformly distributed random numbers between 0 and 1 (@RAND function in a spreadsheet). We'll call them A and B.

2.   Multiply each number by 2, then subtract 1:
$$R_1 = (2 \cdot A) - 1; \quad R_2 = (2 \cdot B) - 1$$

3.   Now calculate the number: $X = (R_1)^2 + (R_2)^2$

4.   If the number X is greater than or equal to 1.00, then go back to step 1 and start over.

5.   If X was less than 1.00, calculate the number:
$$Y = SQRT[-2 \cdot \ln(X)/X]$$

6.   Let $Z_1 = Y \cdot (R_1)$ and $Z_2 = Y \cdot (R_2)$

Z_1 and Z_2 are two independent standard normal random variables. Repeat this 30 times if you need 60 random numbers.

A useful sample macro to accomplish this is in Chapter 14 of *Numerical Techniques in Finance*, Simon Benninga (Cambridge: MIT Press, 1989). A proof of this method is in *The Art of Computer Programming, Vol. 2: Seminumerical Algorithms,* 2nd ed., D.E. Knuth (Reading, MA: Addison-Wesley, 1981).

If your computer software will not generate standard normal random numbers (average of 0, deviation of 1, and a normal distribution), as many will not,[b] then you can formulate your own approximation of a normal random number generator with Lotus 1-2-3, Quattro Pro, or similar software. If you *average up* several of their random numbers (which are distributed *uniformly*, not *normally*), that average will come extremely close to a normal distribution.

Somewhere off to the side of your basic work area on your spreadsheet, put 16 columns of random numbers (@RAND or some similar command) on each of the 60 rows (months)—a 16x60 block of random numbers. Due to the bulk of random numbers that must be recalculated constantly, I recommend setting the spreadsheet's "recalc" mode to manual. You will later hit the "recalc key" for each complete run of the simulation.

You will now create a single column of 60 usable random numbers (one per month) from the 16x60 block of spreadsheet random numbers. We will use the 16 random numbers in each row to create one *standard normal random number*[c] that we can then convert into a monthly stock return. You will average the 16 random numbers in the row, then subtract 0.5 and divide the result by 0.07217.[d] For example, if you had the first row of random numbers in the spreadsheet cells AA1..AP1, then the formula for the first month, which you might place in cell X1, would be:

(@avg(AA1..AP1)-.5)/.07217

Now copy this formula down the rest of the 60-month column. Don't be alarmed if many are negative—about half of them are supposed to be, and almost all of them should fall between -2 and +2. You have now generated a *standard normal random number* for each and every month.

Step 2 is to take the random number and convert it into a monthly stock return that is centered (on average) on 1.25%

and has a deviation (around that center) of 5.5%.[e] This is easy. Simply take each random number you generated, first multiply it by 0.055, and then add 0.0125. For example, since you placed the standard normal random number for the first month in cell X1, the formula for that month's stock return would be:

$$0.055*X1+0.0125$$

Perhaps you will place this formula into cell A1. Then copy this formula down the column so that you have a simulated stock return for each of your 60 months in your first column. You may also want to "format" that range as "percentages," since that is how we commonly think of stock returns. Finally, insert one or more blank rows at the top of the spreadsheet to allow room for month zero and perhaps some column headings.

Step 3 is simple. Next to each stock return, you want the stock price. Start with an index number for month zero[f] (the month before month 1), such as 1.00, or the current level of the Dow Jones Index, or even your uncle's age; the only rule is that you must use a positive number. The price a month later will be the current price times [1 + the monthly return]. Copy this formula down the column; each price calculation will first "reach up" one cell to take the previous price, and then "reach over" to the return column to multiply that previous price by [1+return]. For example, suppose you had added five blank lines to the top of the spreadsheet, so that the month 1 stock return (suppose it is -3%) is in cell A6. We'll put the stock prices in column B and start off with month zero by entering 1.00 in cell B5. Now, next to the -3% return you will program the price for month 1 by entering this formula in cell B6:

$$+B5*(1+A6)$$

A new month 1 price of 0.97 should appear in cell B6 now. Finally, copy this formula down the next 59 cells in column B.

You will now have prices for month zero through 60 in the column range B5..B65.

Check your work to make sure it makes sense. If your monthly return was +10% and the previous price was 2, your new monthly price should now be 2.2. Of course, there should be no negative prices, and the final price should be of a sensible magnitude, given the parameters you choose to use.

Once you've generated monthly returns and prices, you can go to town evaluating any rules or strategy you choose (step 4). Tables 2-1 and 3-1 (on pages 27 and 40 respectively) do this for dollar cost averaging and value averaging (using real, not simulated, prices). For step 5, you may find that writing a macro (a series of instructions that the spreadsheet will follow and repeat as often as you like) is helpful, but you could certainly choose to "recalc" and record the results manually.

ENDNOTES TO APPENDIX TO CHAPTER 7

a.   Or, however many periods you wish to investigate; we'll proceed with 60 periods in this example.

b.   Popular spreadsheet programs such as Lotus 123, Quattro Pro, and Excel, produce *uniformly* distributed random numbers—these are quite different from the *normally* distributed numbers that you will need.

c.   Random numbers created by averaging together 16 numbers with a uniform distribution come close enough to being normally distributed to suffice for purposes of a realistic market simulation. This was checked using the repeated application of a statistical test known as the Studentized Range test for normality.

d.   The averaging "converts" the *uniform* shape into the *normal* shape, as mentioned in the last note. The mean of the resulting number is 0.5 and the standard deviation is $1/(SQRT(12 \cdot N))$, or 0.07217 in the case of $N=16$ random numbers. So you have to deduct the mean of 0.5, and then divide by the deviation of 0.07217. Then, you will have a near-normal random number with a mean of 0 and a deviation of 1.

e.   Of course, in designing your own simulation, you may use your own parameters for center and spread. If you plan to do this, or to change the parameters at any time, it is good spreadsheet programming practice to use absolute cell references to "point to" the cells containing those values, as opposed to typing the values directly into the formula as is done in the text.

f.   If you haven't left any room at the top of the spreadsheet, you may need to insert a row for month 0.

Comparing the Strategies 8

This chapter looks at hundreds of simulated markets (as described in Chapter 7) to evaluate dollar cost averaging, value averaging, and several variations that have already been discussed. We have already accomplished this comparison in Chapters 2–6 using actual historical market data. The results you will see using market simulations should not surprise you too much. These results should, however, give you a much better feel for how the various strategies do under different circumstances that you have not seen or been able to evaluate with the historical data. This type of simulated comparison is useful in answering typical questions that interested readers tend to have.

FIVE-YEAR SIMULATION RESULTS

The first 100 simulated runs of our five-year random market (as shown in Figure 7-2) were used to evaluate the dollar cost averaging and value averaging strategies in their "pure" or "fixed-amount" forms. The rates of return are displayed, ordered worst to best from left to right in Figure 8-1. This is *not* a time-series. You are *not* looking at how an investment evolves over 100 consecutive periods; instead, each symbol represents the rate of return over a separate, complete 5-year simulated investment. For each simulation, the vertical position of the line shows the IRR (rate of return) for dollar cost averaging, and the symbol above or below the line shows the IRR with value averaging. The rate of return with value averaging exceeds that with dollar cost averaging (i.e., the symbol is above the line) on

Figure 8-1 COMPARISON OF RATES OF RETURN

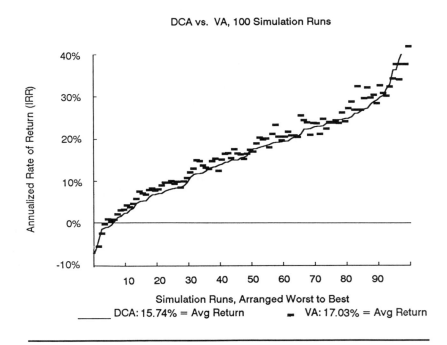

DCA vs. VA, 100 Simulation Runs

A comparison of the rates of return of DCA and VA, using the 100 different simulated markets (runs) from Figure 7-2. They are ordered "bear-to-bull," so you can see more easily the return difference.

84 out of 100 occasions. The average of all 100 rates of return from each strategy are shown in the legend of the figure: value averaging returned 17.03% on average, compared to 15.74% with dollar cost averaging, and 15.23% with the constant share strategy (not shown). The average returns were slightly more variable (riskier) with the DCA strategy.[1] The best relative performance of value averaging was a +6.05% higher return than DCA; the worst of the 16 losers was -3.09% lower than DCA. Over these 100 simulated 5-year markets, the final share price ended up lower than it started on six occasions   (as was

Figure 8-2 COMPARISON OF RATES OF RETURN

DCA vs. VA, 2nd 100 Simulation Runs

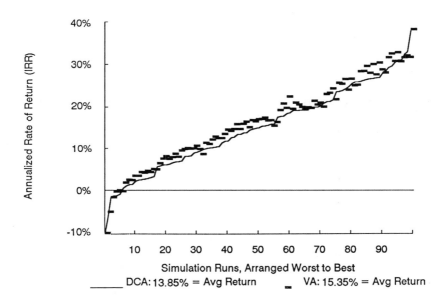

Simulation Runs, Arranged Worst to Best

_____ DCA: 13.85% = Avg Return   ▬ VA: 15.35% = Avg Return

This is the same comparison as above, except that a different 100 simulated market runs are used (from Figure 7-3 instead of 7-2). The "pure" $100-a-month versions of each strategy are used.

noted in Figure 7-2). The CS strategy provided negative returns 7 times, dollar cost averaging was negative 6 times, and the value averaging strategy had negative returns only 3 times out of 100 simulations.

Figure 8-2 shows exactly the same exact comparison as in Figure 8-1, except that the *second* 100 runs of the random simulation, instead of the first 100 (as previously shown in Figure 7-3) are used as the basis of comparison. This time, value averaging has returns that average 1.50 percentage points higher (15.35% over 13.85%) than dollar cost averaging, and it has higher returns 90 times out of the 100 simulations shown.

When this comparison of the pure strategies was repeated again and again using different runs of the simulation, the results were not terribly different. Table 8-1 shows the average results for the first three different 100-runs of the simulation.

Table 8-1 Comparison of "Pure" Strategies First 3 Sets of 100 Runs of Simulation					
Simulation Runs	Average IRR (Annual Rate of Return)			VA – DCA Extremes	
	CS	DCA	VA	Worst	Best
1st 100	15.23%	15.74%	17.03%	-3.09%	+6.05%
2nd 100	13.23%	13.85%	15.35%	-1.22%	+3.83%
3rd 100	14.34%	14.88%	16.28%	-3.30%	+5.22%

On average over hundreds of simulation runs, the formula strategies do better than a CS strategy; value averaging does the best, with VA beating out DCA by about a 1.4% return on average. The last 2 columns list worst and best return differences between VA and DCA, with a positive difference meaning that VA had the higher annual return by that much over a particular 5-year simulation.

The table further shows that value averaging tends to outperform dollar cost averaging by over a 1% higher return, whereas dollar cost averaging outperforms constant share purchases by about one-half point. Only rarely was the return difference between strategies in a given simulation extreme; the wildest (6.05% better for VA, 3.30% better for DCA) return differences are shown in the last 2 columns. Whereas value averaging outperformed dollar cost averaging in only 84 out of the first 100 runs, it was best on 90 and 89 occasions (respectively) over the next two sets of 100 runs of the simulation. You may recall from Chapter 3 that the relative comparison for historical data had a similar score, in that value averaging had "won" 52 of the last 62 overlapping 5-year investment periods.

Figure 8-3 COMPARISON OF RATES OF RETURN

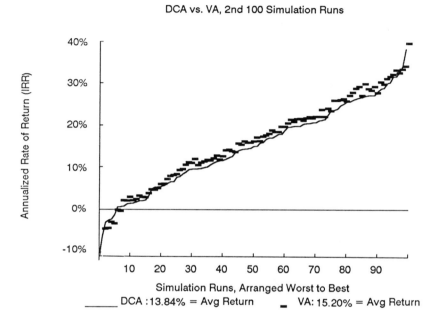

DCA vs. VA, 2nd 100 Simulation Runs

Same simulations as Figure 8-2, except that a monthly growth path of 1.3% (roughly the expected return on the market) is used for both strategies. VA "wins" 92 out of 100 times.

The simulation results show that you could expect slightly better than this historical result out of value averaging in the future.

Using Growth Adjustments

Having compared the strategies in their so-called pure forms, we now look at how they perform when adjusted for expected market growth (as recommended in Chapters 4 and 5). Figure 8-3 shows the performance of the strategies over the second 100 simulation runs, where each strategy used a growth factor of 1.3% per month.[2] Growth adjustments have little effect on the returns from dollar cost averaging; the effect on value averaging is mixed.[3] The number of times the value averaging strategy has the higher rate of return increases to 92 times out of 100. Due to the compounding increase (growth adjustment) of the value path, the variation of returns (the risk) increases slightly with a growth-adjusted value averaging strategy.

Figure 8-4 is exactly like Figure 8-3, except that the performance of the strategies is evaluated over the *third* 100 simulation runs, again using a growth factor of 1.3% per month.

Both strategies perform better (after growth adjustment) over this set of simulations; both increase in average absolute return by about 0.125%. Value averaging outperforms dollar cost averaging on 96 out of 100 runs, compared with to only 87 runs using the same simulations but without any growth adjustments.

When this comparison of the growth-adjusted strategies was repeated again and again using different runs of the simulation, the results were not terribly different. Table 8-2 shows the average results for the first three different 100-runs of the simulation.

Table 8-2 Comparison of "Growth-Adjusted" Strategies First 3 Sets of 100 Runs of Simulation					
Simulation Runs	Average IRR (Rate of Return)			# times VA beat DCA	
	CS	DCA	VA	Pure	Grow Adj
1st 100	15.23%	15.87%	17.13%	84	92
2nd 100	13.23%	13.84%	15.20%	90	92
3rd 100	14.34%	15.01%	16.41%	89	96

The last 2 columns show that the probability of beating the return of dollar cost averaging with value averaging is higher if the value path is growth adjusted.

There seem to be theoretical, performance, and common-sense reasons for applying some growth adjustment to whatever formula strategy you use. Higher rates of growth (in the amount you invest), which exceeded even the most optimistic expected market returns, were also analyzed. The numbers (not shown) weren't terribly different from what you see in Table 8-2, and there appears to be little return advantage to using extreme growth levels in planning your investment quantities. As you might suspect, both strategies are made riskier by the use of above-market growth factors, and value averaging is affected the most in that respect.

Figure 8-4 COMPARISON OF RATES OF RETURN

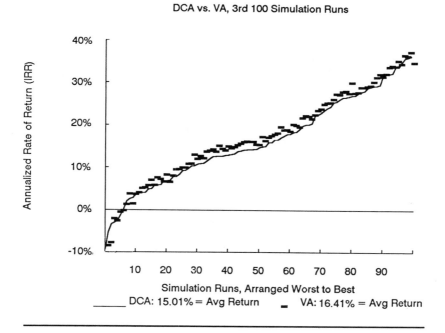

DCA vs. VA, 3rd 100 Simulation Runs

Simulation Runs, Arranged Worst to Best

_____ DCA: 15.01% = Avg Return ▬ VA: 16.41% = Avg Return

Just like Figure 8-3, a 1.3% growth adjustment is used for both strategies. Here, though, a different 3rd set of 100 random simulated markets is used to evaluate the strategies. VA "wins" 96 out of 100.

No-Sell Variation

Chapter 6 discussed the possibility of doing nothing when the value averaging strategy "dictates" selling shares, and analyzed that variation using actual market data. Figure 8-5 displays the results of *no-sell* value averaging compared to dollar cost averaging in exactly the same scenario as in Figure 8-3. Both strategies are growth adjusted, and the second set of 100 simulations is used.

Figure 8-5 COMPARISON OF RATES OF RETURN

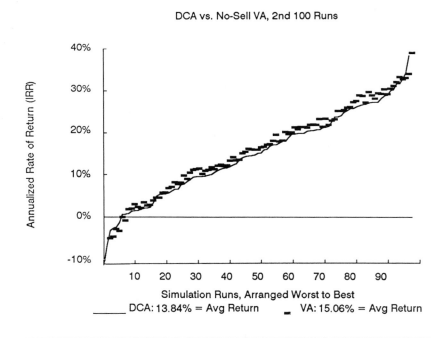

DCA vs. No-Sell VA, 2nd 100 Runs

Simulation Runs, Arranged Worst to Best

_____ DCA: 13.84% = Avg Return   ▬ VA: 15.06% = Avg Return

This is just like Figure 8-3, except that now the *no-sell* variation of the VA strategy is used. Both DCA and VA still use 1.3% growth factors.

As suspected, failing to follow the sell recommendations of the value averaging strategy did have an adverse impact on performance—but not as much as you might suspect. In the simulation shown, the reduction in average annual return was only -0.14%; in the other two hundred simulations the reduction was -0.18% and -0.16%. By using the no-sell variant, you are only giving up about one-eighth of the return advantage of the value averaging strategy.

Volatility

By straying from the expected market parameters of center and spread discussed in the previous chapter, we can begin to understand how volatility affects the relative performance of the strategies. Because value averaging operates by taking advantage of large moves in either direction, you might suspect that the relative return advantage of value averaging will increase with volatility.

Some simulations are performed for markets with only half the typical volatility, and then with double volatility. If the standard deviation of monthly returns is reduced to 2.75% (half of the 5.5% figure used throughout this chapter), the average relative return advantage of value averaging diminishes significantly (but is still positive). When the volatility is 11%, or double the normal figure, the return difference between strategies increases substantially. The average rate of return advantage of a pure value averaging strategy over 100 simulation runs in these situations is:

- +0.38% with half the volatility;
- +1.50% with standard volatility; and
- +5.76% with double volatility.

Figure 8-6 COMPARISON OF RATES OF RETURN

DCA vs. VA, Market Volatility x 2

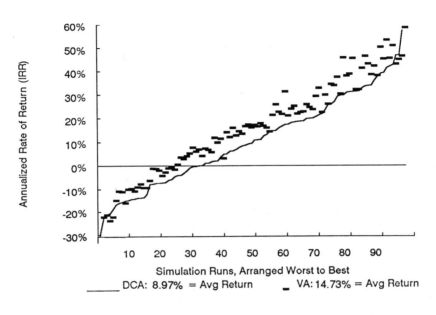

Strategies are checked under *extreme volatility*. This shows the "pure" strategies as in Figure 8-2, but now the simulation uses *twice* the market volatility. Average market price increase was 8.35%.

Results of the double volatility simulation are presented in Figure 8-6. In this simulation, the pure value averaging strategy averaged an annualized return of 14.73%, compared with the return of 8.97% with dollar cost averaging, and only 6.62% for constant share purchases (not shown). The largest return advantage out of the 100 runs was a +15.67% difference between value averaging and dollar cost averaging; the worst performance was a -2.86% decrease in return due to value averaging. In 94 of the 100 simulations, value averaging came out on top. When this experiment was repeated again with another 100 different simulation runs, there was a 5.83%

average return advantage for value averaging, which "won" on 97 out of 100 runs. Changing the strategies by adjusting for growth and by not selling did not make the results any better for value averaging than what we have just seen.

All the strategies obviously became riskier when volatility increases. Interestingly, although the relative risk of value averaging does increase (over DCA) a bit with volatility, it is not a very significant increase. Still, the fact is that value averaging results in less investment exposure and value than dollar cost averaging portfolios when prices go way up, and in more investment exposure when prices go way down. Thus, it is still important to pick out a diversified investment vehicle (to avoid bankruptcy risk) with which to implement value averaging or any other contrarian[4] formula strategy.

TWENTY-YEAR SIMULATION RESULTS

Absolute or total market volatility increases over time,[5] so you might suspect that the relative return advantage of value averaging would increase substantially over time. It does not seem to. A 20-year simulated market was constructed, and investments were made at 4-month intervals using the standard annual market return parameters. A growth adjustment of 5% per period (about 15% per year) was applied to both strategies. The results are represented in Figure 8-7.

Over 100 runs of the simulated market, the value averaging strategy outperformed dollar cost averaging 96 times. The compound average annual return for value averaging was 15.59%, comparing favorably with 14.31% for dollar cost averaging, and 13.66% for constant share purchases (not shown). The relative effectiveness of value averaging is related to the volatility *per unit time*.

Figure 8-7 COMPARISON OF RATES OF RETURN

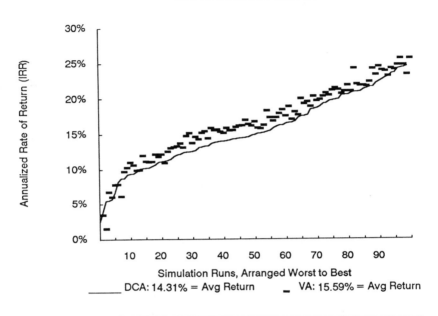

DCA vs. VA, 20-Year Simulations

Annualized Rate of Return (IRR)

Simulation Runs, Arranged Worst to Best

DCA: 14.31% = Avg Return   VA: 15.59% = Avg Return

This 20-year simulation uses only 3 investment periods per year, spaced every 4 months and using a 5% growth rate. VA "beat" DCA 96 out of 100 times.

SUMMARY

We've just "paper-traded" several variations of the investment strategies to see how they would perform under a wide range of plausible market conditions. Under these simulations, in most cases value averaging performs better than the other strategies and gives higher returns on average. The market simulation was a true "random walk," so conceivably these results could be expected in real markets. This is really true only if stock market returns are truly *random*. This point will be discussed at length in Chapter 9.

ENDNOTES

1. The variation of the returns gives you some sense of the risk involved in the strategies. The standard deviation of the 100 annualized 5-year returns was 11.16% for dollar cost averaging and 10.73% for value averaging. Although value averaging was the less-risky strategy here, it was about equivalent in risk to dollar cost averaging on average, over the total of thousands of simulations done on different variations using different runs of market prices.

2. The dollar cost averaging strategy used a growing monthly investment amount, increasing the original $100 investment at 1.3% per month. Value averaging used a 1.3% growth factor as described in Chapter 5. The value path for month *t* was:

$$V_t = 100 \times t \times (1 + 0.013)^t$$

Thus, the value path started at $100 and grew to $13,023 over the 5-year period.

3. In this case, the average effect of growth adjusting is to decrease the average relative advantage and absolute return on value averaging (from 15.35% to 15.20%). Over more simulations, growth adjusting (on average) tends to increase the absolute return on value averaging, with no effect or perhaps an insignificant decrease in the *relative* return advantage on value averaging over dollar cost averaging.

4. Contrarian strategies invest in something that is out of favor. Formula strategies such as value averaging are contrarian across time, investing the most in the market when it is in the least favor (prices are low), cutting against the popular investment trend.

5. It is much more likely that the price of a $100 stock is outside a range of $80–$120 after a decade than after a month. This "total volatility" is a different concept than "annualized" or average volatility, which decreases over time (as you saw in previous chapters). As time increases, *total* volatility increases by the square root of time, but *average* volatility per period *decreases* by the square root of time. A simplified example: If the standard deviation of return over *1* year is 20%, what happens over a *4*-year period? The square root of the time increase (four) is two. So *total* volatility over the entire 4-year period doubles to 40%; thus, *average* volatility each year is halved to 10% per year.

Profiting 9
from Overreaction

Ongoing research in the financial academic community may directly support the wisdom of formula strategies in general, especially contrarian formula strategies like value averaging. The bottom line of this research, in layperson's terms, is that *prices in financial markets possibly overreact.*

TIRING OF A RANDOM WALK

This unimposing and seemingly innocuous observation packs an enormous punch if in fact it is true. It flies in the face of earlier theories that stock market and other financial market prices follow a *random walk*. Basically, the random walk hypothesis states that a series or daily, monthly, or annual rates of return on the market are uncorrelated, much like the sequential outcomes of the flip of a coin or the roll of the dice. That is, what happened today really tells you nothing about what will happen in tomorrow's market. Although this *efficient market*[1] view is far from being accepted universally in the investment community, few have quarreled with its main precepts: new information affecting stocks is readily and efficiently reflected in prices; higher returns come at the cost of higher risk; and past results can't predict future performance.[2]

Kenneth R. French, who has done much research with Eugene Fama on stock price movements, notes: "Until recently, most financial economists agreed that stock returns are essentially unpredictable."[3] In the late 1980s, much evidence was analyzed to shed a different light on the movements of prices in various stock markets in over a dozen countries. As a result, few economists now believe that stock prices follow a strict random walk. It is still a good approximation for individual stocks over very short time periods; however, there is increasing evidence of *mean reversion* (defined below) in stock prices over periods of about two to four years.[4]

In using dividend yields as one method of checking on the predictability of market returns, French and Fama summarized: "The predictability of returns in our dividend yield regressions and in [similar works by others] is striking. A number of researchers are currently exploring the implications of this predictability for economic models and financial applications."[5] Professor Stewart C. Myers of MIT comments on another study: "Poterba and Summers have accumulated an impressive amount of evidence for mean reversion. . . . Stock returns appear to be mean reverting."[6]

Mean Reversion and Overreaction

Mean reversion means that the market overreacts in the short run but generally can be counted on to "correct itself" in the longer run. In the *Wall Street Journal*, Barbara Donnelly writes, "Taking a page from experimental psychology, the investor behaviorists argue that people overreact to unexpected or dramatic news events, especially negative ones, causing prices to fall further than they should. But those prices, according to studies of stock market performance, invariably rebound as the pendulum of market sentiment reverses."[7]

"It's as if there's a law of gravity in stock prices," says Lawrence Summers, a professor of economics at Harvard University who has studied these patterns. "The market," he continues, "is ultimately anchored in fundamentals, so any irrational price movement away from those fundamental values has got to be eventually reversed."[8] Thus, the behaviorists conclude, investors who keep their heads in the face of bad news and big price drops stand to reap real benefits.

Perhaps one of the more compelling examples of this is the apparent overreaction that came both before and during the Black Monday stock market crash on October 19, 1987. Wild-eyed optimism and bull market greed fed the seemingly irrational and lofty levels of the market for a short time. Then, as the market "corrected," a short-term panic set in that drove the market too far in the opposite direction. That same week the market had one of its best days in history, correcting much of the Black Monday overreaction. Like a spring that oscillates wildly at first but eventually settles in on itself, the market's reactions dampened until its price level more closely reflected its fundamentally supportable level. Any markets driven by investor psychology (in addition to fundamental values) has the potential to exhibit these characteristics. Anyone who has followed the news over the past decade can think of several regular episodes of commodity price overreaction followed by mean reversion. Several distinctly memorable episodes from the 1980s involve gold, silver, platinum, orange juice, coffee, copper, and, most recently, oil. Already in the 1990s, the roller-coaster Japanese stock market shows evidence of joining this club of dubious distinction.

To get a better feel for how the stock market may overreact and mean revert, we now turn to analyzing market data for periods of varying lengths.

A Brief Look at the Data

The predictability of market returns has been found to depend greatly on the time period in question. Poterba and Summers[9] found a substantial tendency for the various stock markets to overreact in the short term (days, weeks, and months) but to mean revert, or correct the overreactions, in the long term (a year or longer periods). Other recent studies support these findings.

Most of these studies have used effective but complex statistical methods that are inaccessible to most people. I have presented the results of my own "quick and dirty" study on market returns below, using rather basic techniques that I hope you will follow and find interesting.

Suppose the market really followed a random walk, almost like a series of coin flips. First, it is important to note that the "market coin" is not a "fair" coin, because the market goes up more than down (as, of course, it should). So imagine a weighted coin that comes up heads 60% of the time and tails 40% of the time. Now if the coin comes up heads this time, that gives us no advance information on what it will come up next time. That is, if we get heads now, there's still a 60-40 chance we'll get another heads tomorrow. If we'd gotten tails now, there still would be a 60-40 chance we'd get heads tomorrow. Likewise, in *either* case there's a 40-60 chance we'll get tails —regardless of what happened on the previous flip. The random walk hypothesis is that market returns from period to period will be *independent*, just like the coin flips above. Using this basic story, I set up an experiment using stock market return data from the 1926–1991 period (or 1962–1991 for daily data only), described below.

Looking at the market return for each period (let's use *months* as an example), we classify the return for each period as either *above* or *below* average.[10] Please see Table 9-1, which presents the results for the monthly period experiment. You can see that the average monthly return was +0.95%. Next, we look from each period to the next, seeing how returns match up in consecutive months. Four outcomes are possible, listed here with the actual number of occurrences (out of 791):

1. Above-average month followed by another above-average month (228);
2. Above-average month followed by a below-average month (185);
3. Below-average month followed by an above average-month (186)[11];

4. Below-average month followed by another below-average month (192).

Outcomes 1 and 4 are classified as a period-to-period MATCH (as the good or bad market "persists"), and outcomes 2 and 3 are classified as a SWITCH (good market turns bad, or vice versa). The way the experiment is set up, you would expect about as many MATCHES as SWITCHES if the market followed a random walk. If not, then each period's market outcome gives you a little information about *next* period's market return. Not enough information to make millions of dollars with, but plenty more information than we expected!

TABLE 9-1 Consecutive-Period Performance of the Stock Market			
Monthly Periods n = 791 AVG = 0.95%		Return on the Market *This* Month	
		Above AVG	Below AVG
Return on the Market *Last* Month	Above AVG	228_{MATCH}	185_{SWITCH}
	Below AVG	186_{SWITCH}	192_{MATCH}

In 53.1% of the periods analyzed, the market return MATCHED that of the previous period. That is, well over half the time above-average months were followed by above-average months, with below-average months followed by below average months.[12]

In the monthly case shown in Table 9-1, there are 420 MATCHES and only 371 SWITCHES—a 53.1% chance of "persistence" in market returns, more than the roughly 50% you would expect. This means that the market "overreacts" from month to month, tending to roll with its momentum in the direction in which it's already headed. The statistical significance of these occurences is summarized in the the table endnote.

Because the Great Depression is included in the data, I split the data in each experiment into halves, 1926–1958 and 1959–1991. Separate tables with the results are not presented, but in the monthly case, the MATCH percentages were 56% for the early half and 51% for the later half. The overreaction seems stronger prior to 1958, but there still seem to be monthly overreactions, no matter which period we look at.

The next experiments were performed on quarterly stock returns. In Table 9-2a, we look at standard quarters (those ending on 31 March, 30 June, 30 September, and 31 December). The MATCH percentage is given in the table note, showing that 52.5% of the 263 quarter-to-quarter stock returns stayed the same.

TABLE 9-2a Consecutive-Period Performance of the Stock Market			
Quarterly Periods (End of Mar/Jun/Sep/Dec) n = 263 AVG = 3.04%		Return on the Market *This* Quarter	
		Above AVG	Below AVG
Return on the Market *Last* Quarter	Above AVG	80	62
	Below AVG	63	58

In 52.5% of the periods analyzed, the market return MATCHED that of the previous period.

It doesn't much matter how you split the months into quarters to do the experiment. To show this, Table 9-2b shows the same experiment, running the quarters on a January-April-July-October cycle, and Table 9-2c uses the third possible cycle for dividing up the quarters.

Results are similar. On the second quarterly cycle, there is a MATCH percentage of 51.9%; on the third and final cycle (Table 9-2c), a MATCH percentage of almost exactly 50%.

TABLE 9-2b Consecutive-Period Performance of the Stock Market			
Quarterly Periods (End of Jan/Apr/Jul/Oct) n = 262 AVG = 2.78%		Return on the Market *This* Quarter	
		Above AVG	Below AVG
Return on the Market *Last* Quarter	Above AVG	78	63
	Below AVG	63	58

In 51.9% of the periods analyzed, the market return MATCHED that of the previous period.

TABLE 9-2c Consecutive-Period Performance of the Stock Market			
Quarterly Periods (End of Feb/May/Aug/Nov) n = 262 AVG = 3.05%		Return on the Market *This* Quarter	
		Above AVG	Below AVG
Return on the Market *Last* Quarter	Above AVG	67	66
	Below AVG	66	63

In 49.6% of the periods analyzed, the market return MATCHED that of the previous period.

The combined average quarterly percentage is 51.3% quarter-to-quarter MATCHES.[13] Overall, quarterly returns exhibit a mild persistence or overreaction, but not enough to be statistically significant or terribly convincing.

We are starting to see a pattern of less overreaction as the time period gets longer. This continues as we look at annual returns over the 1926–1991 time frame, in Table 9-3. The average annual return on the market was 12.03%, and there were 65 year-to-year pairs. Only 46.2% of these consecutive year returns were MATCHES—the first figure we've seen substantially under 50%.[14] You will note here, and also in the biennial experiments to follow, that long-term, below-average market returns are *extremely nonpersistent*. After a bad year, only 11 of 29 (38%) of the following years would also turn out bad. The similar figure for back-to-back, two-year periods is 40%. After seeing these numbers, you should be thinking about the potential returns to "gutting it out" in a bad market and questioning the irrational human nature (or *lemming* nature?) to bail out while the market seems to be heading south.

TABLE 9-3 Consecutive-Period Performance of the Stock Market			
Annual Periods n = 65 AVG = 12.03%		Return on the Market *This* Period	
		Above AVG	Below AVG
Return on the Market *Last* Period	Above AVG	19	17
	Below AVG	18	11

In 46.2% of the periods analyzed, the market return MATCHED that of the previous period. So, unlike the short-term returns above, annual returns tend to *NOT* MATCH those of the previous period.[15]

The year-to-year numbers display what we call *mean reversion*. Whereas momentum seemed to carry market levels careening off in one direction in the short term, there appears to be a long-term "spring" attached to stocks that pulls market overreactions back to some long-term trend—not as a rule, but certainly more often than not.

These tendencies are even more evident when the length of time is extended to two-year periods. Consecutive two-year periods are analyzed, starting both in odd years (December

1925–December 1927, for example) in Table 9-4a, and in even years in Table 9-4b.

TABLE 9-4a Consecutive-Period Performance of the Stock Market			
Two-Year Periods (Odd-numbered Years) n = 32 AVG = 24.94%		Return on the Market *This* Period	
		Above AVG	Below AVG
Return on the Market *Last* Period	Above AVG	6	10
	Below AVG	9	7

In only 40.6% of the periods analyzed, the market return MATCHED that of the previous period.

Here, the mean-reverting tendencies of long-term stock returns are even more evident. The MATCH percentages are 40.6% and 38.7%, depending on how you carve out the two-year periods. The combined average two-year period percentage is only 39.7% MATCHES.[16] The persistence of short-term market returns seems to be seriously corrected over longer and longer periods.

TABLE 9-4b Consecutive-Period Performance of the Stock Market			
Two-Year Periods (Even-numbered Years) n = 31 AVG = 25.88%		Return on the Market *This* Period	
		Above AVG	Below AVG
Return on the Market *Last* Period	Above AVG	7	10
	Below AVG	9	5

In only 38.7% of the periods analyzed, the market return MATCHED that of the previous period.

The following information on consecutive returns from day to day are provided in Table 9-5. They are based on a different data set (1962–1991), because daily data are not readily available for 1926–1961.

TABLE 9-5 Consecutive-Period Performance of the Stock Market			
Daily Periods (since July 1962) n = 7418 AVG = 0.0460%		Return on the Market *Today*	
		Above AVG	Below AVG
Return on the Market *Yesterday*	Above AVG	2,178	1,600
	Below AVG	1,600	2,040

In 56.9% of the days analyzed, the market return MATCHED that of the previous period.[17]

The short-term persistence of market returns is phenomenal at the daily level—tomorrow's return is quite likely to have the same characteristic as today's return.

To put all this in perspective, we can line up the MATCH percentages for each time period analyzed (see Table 9-6) to see the same clear pattern that other researchers have also found with more scientific methods. Although not all of these results are significantly different from 50% (statistically speaking), the overall pattern is quite hard to dispute. It clearly could not be coincidence that short-term overreactions so gradually and consistently turn into long-term mean reversion.

This makes some logical sense, as well. If, for example, positive daily and monthly overreactions tend to pile up over a year causing a rather high market level, but the market and its investors are rational in the long run, then you would suspect

TABLE 9-6 Review of Period-to-Period Return MATCHES *(50% is expected in a "random walk" market)*[18]		
Day to day	56.9%	Short-term Overreaction
Month to month	53.1%	.
Quarter to quarter	51.3%	:
Year to year	46.2%	:
Two-year periods	39.7%	Long-term Mean Reversion

The percentage figure shown is the proportion of times that a market return for a given period had the same mean characteristic (that is, *above-* or *below-*average) as the period before. Note that short-term returns tend to MATCH the previous return, while long-term returns tend to SWITCH from period to period.

some tendency for a below-average return next year to correct the first year's market overreaction. Some overreactions will correct within a year and some will take longer, so you would expect the incidence of SWITCHING over the longer consecutive two-year periods to be even more pronounced than for annual periods. This story is supported by the data.

The data analyzed here and in the more sophisticated academic studies do not *prove* that markets overreact or mean revert. It is *highly likely* that they do, but hard to prove beyond the shadow of a doubt without even more data. Professor Myers points out in *Frontiers of Finance* that, even after years of study the data may be fairly convincing but not conclusive: "The evidence for medium-term mean reversion in stock returns is not universally accepted, however. Stock prices are extremely noisy, and there are not that many non-overlapping 4-year [medium-term] time periods."[19]

WHY DOES THIS MATTER?

It should be clear by now why market overreaction can be a good thing. At a most basic level, the mean-reverting characteristic of the market means that long-term investors face less risk than previously thought. But more relevant to your investment plans is the fact that formula strategies can almost automatically take advantage of market overreactions, because they generally move you "against" the market at its extremes. So when the market moves into "irrational zones," that is, away from its fundamental value, formula strategies such as value averaging guide you to take advantage of the potentially temporary high price by getting out (or of the low price by buying) before the overreaction is corrected. Of course, no system can distinguish a price that has made a large move due to overreaction from one that is due to a genuine permanent movement in fundamental value.

A year or so after publication of the original "Value Averaging" article, many of the investors who wrote me had actually been using the strategy in various ways after reading about it. They all reported better results (relative to dollar cost averaging) than would have been predicted by simulation studies. Of course, it was hard to read too much into this, given the well-above-average market performance around 1989. But we have also seen, in previous chapters, that the incremental return to value averaging could indeed be higher in *real* historical markets than in average *simulated* markets. This is particularly true when using 3-month or 4-month intervals for value averaging; it is less clear at monthly intervals. The additional relative return of VA in real markets (as compared to simulated markets) is possibly due to the apparent overreaction of actual *historical* market prices—the *simulated* market series were designed as a true random walk, without any overreacting or mean-reverting characteristics.

If markets do indeed overreact, then a formula strategy, by working against temporary overpricing or underpricing, may exceed the returns for other investment methods, even after adjustment for risk.[20] In a pure random walk market, no purely mechanical investment strategy can "add value" in an economic sense. But if the market deviates from a random walk (as it seems to), then value actually may be added (typical risk-return trade-offs can be enhanced) with a mechanical formula strategy.

There's no real downside (on average) to trying to glean a minor advantage over the market in this way. Even if the data were just a mirage and the market really was and always would be a random walk, then we are only right back where we started (as in previous chapters), with a disciplined and workable approach to the market that gets us a fair return for the risk taken with our investment dollar. Recall the important point that the value averaging strategy provided higher investment returns even when a pure random walk (with no overreaction) simulation was used—deviations from the random walk could only improve the situation.

Timing

Now we can think about how best to time a strategy so as to take advantage of market overreaction. If we try to use value averaging to take advantage of the extreme highs and lows of overreaction, *how often* should we "revalue" our portfolio to buy or sell stock?

A sensible guess can be derived from the "matching percentage" data in Table 9-6. Think about each extreme. Would *daily* value averaging make sense? No. Suppose there's a big move *up* in the market. With value averaging, we'd sell shares. But the 56.9% MATCH ratio means that tomorrow is likely to be a big market day as well. We'd have sold a bit prematurely in that the market is still undergoing possible short-term overreaction. At the other extreme, suppose we entered the market only every two years with value averaging. If we had a very good two-year period, the next period is more likely to be a bad one. Thus, the selling recommended by the value averaging formula would seem to make sense. But the market was also "correcting" overreactions over a shorter one-year period as well. If the market is mean reverting over one-year periods, there are gains to be made by entering the market every year, as opposed to every other year. That is, value averaging every two years wouldn't get us out quickly enough —in time to take advantage of the full expected market correction (mean reversion). While value averaging during a mean-reverting period is good, it's not as good as using a *shorter* period (that is also mean reverting).

There must be some optimal middle ground. We don't want to set our value averaging at a time frequency where the market is overreacting (too early), or where the market is mean reverting (too late). If the market overreacts over short periods and mean reverts over long periods, there is some medium-length time period over which market returns are (on average) a random walk. From the data in Table 9-6, this appears to be roughly quarterly or a little longer. It would seem that value averaging two, three, or four times a year would be reasonable possible strategies for milking the most out of the VA strategy.

We can do better than just looking at the matching percentages. By actually testing the formula strategies over historical market data, we can see how the advantage to value averaging varies, depending on the frequency of the time period we used. I show the results of this experiment for two time periods in the tables below. In Table 9-7, the period July 1962 to December 1991 is used, so that daily data can be analyzed as well as longer periods. Table 9-8 looks at the entire 1926–1991 period, but only at monthly and greater frequencies. The results of three strategies are shown. The first is the rate of return on constant share purchases (CS), or purchasing a "share" of the market each period. The returns resulting from growth-equalized[21] dollar cost averaging and value averaging strategies are

Table 9-7 Rate of Return Using Various Investment Frequencies: July 1962–December 1991					
Investment Frequency	CS	DCA	VA	Advantage of VA over:	
	%	%	%	CS	DCA
Daily	12.26	12.64	13.39	+1.13%	+0.75%
5-Day Period	12.26	12.64	13.56	+1.30	+0.92
Monthly	12.30	12.72	13.61	+1.31	+0.89
Quarterly	12.24	12.72	13.77	+1.53	+1.05
Yearly	12.16	12.35	12.95	+0.79	+0.60
2-Year Period	11.99	12.13	12.31	+0.32	+0.18

Annualized internal rate of return for each strategy if using the investment frequency shown.

also shown. The return is shown for each investment frequency evaluated, stated in annualized terms for consistency.

The results of the limited data set used for Table 9-7 show that the intuition about frequency timing described above was indeed correct. The optimal strategy turned out (after the fact) to be a *quarterly* frequency for value averaging;[22] this yielded a +1.53% improvement over CS and +1.05% improvement over the DCA strategy.

In summary, no one knows exactly how the market really moves; nor can we predict the future or even whether it will be much like the past. But evidence seems to indicate that the market has a tendency (on average) to overreact in the short term and then to mean revert over some longer term. Formula strategies that play on temporary possible market mispricings are a reasonable way of taking advantage of overreactions. Using value averaging with a quarterly investment frequency has, in the

Table 9-8 Rate of Return Using Various Investment Frequencies: 1926–1991					
Investment Frequency	CS	DCA	VA	Advantage of VA over:	
	%	%	%	CS	DCA
Monthly	11.24	11.46	12.56	+1.32%	+1.09%
Quarterly	11.09	11.40	12.77	+1.68	+1.37
Yearly	11.23	11.43	12.56	+1.33	+1.13
2-Year Period	11.30	11.41	12.25	+0.95	+0.84

Annualized internal rate of return for each strategy if using the investment frequency shown. Quarterly figures are actually the average of quarterly figures using each of the 3 possible quarterly cycles.

past, yielded higher returns than other strategies and frequencies analyzed.

The full data set shown in Table 9-8 supports the analysis above. The best relative results (+1.37% return advantage) were achieved by using value averaging with a quarterly frequency. In tests over various time periods, value averaging historically has worked very well when done at a frequency of 3, 4, or 6 times a year (every two, three, or four months). A monthly frequency is never much worse, but why go to extra trouble to get a lower average return?

ENDNOTES

1.   This is not quite the same as a similar but more general notion of market prices, known as *market efficiency*; these finer distinctions are beyond the scope of this book.

2.   Barbara Donnelly, "Investors' Overreactions May Yield Opportunities in the Stock Market," *Wall Street Journal,* 7 Jan 1988.

3.   In Stewart C. Myers and Deborah H. Miller, eds., *Frontiers of Finance: The Batterymarch Fellowship Papers.* Cambridge: Blackwell, 1990, p. 511.

4.   Myers, in Myers & Miller, p. 511.

5.   In Myers & Miller, p. 511.

6.   Myers, referring to James M. Poterba and Lawrence H. Summers, "Mean Reversion in Stock Prices: Evidence and Implications," in Myers & Miller, p. 541.

7.   Barbara Donnelly, *Wall Street Journal,* 7 Jan 1988.

8.   Quoted by Barbara Donnelly, "Investors' Overreactions May Yield Opportunities in the Stock Market," *Wall Street Journal,* 7 Jan 1988.

9.   James M. Poterba and Lawrence H. Summers, "Mean Reversion in Stock Prices: Evidence and Implications," *Journal of Financial Economics,* 22 No. 1 (1988), 27–60.

10.   Whereas this approach doesn't seem as intuitive as simply looking at *positive* and *negative* returns, it is a bit easier to work with. No matter what the length of the period, the market return is just about as likely to be *above* average as *below* average; this more closely resembles a fair coin for each experiment. This is *not* true for the positive/negative distinction, because the market tends to rise, especially over longer periods. In any case, the resulting conclusions are *not* sensitive to which technique is used.

11.   As you will see in the tables that follow, outcomes 2 and 3 must necessarily be equal in quantity or, at most, one occurence apart. This is because they are "legs" of a "round trip," where every SWITCH *up* eventually must be followed by one SWITCH *down*, and vice versa.

12.   If you are familiar with basic statistical tests, this result is statistically significant at a 0.10 level, but not at a 0.05 level (p-value of Chi-squared is about 0.07). That means that it is unlikely (a less than 1-in-10 chance) that we could have gotten this result from a "random-walk" market.

13.   The quarterly figures were not very sensitive to the time period used (pre-1958 versus post-1958).

14.   The annual return MATCH percentage was critically dependent on the time period. Before 1958, 17 of 32 consecutive years (53.1%) were a MATCH. After 1958, only 13 of 33 (39.4%) were a MATCH. Using the 39.4% figure for the current time period would only strengthen the conclusions reached herein.

15.   The annual and quarterly results are not statistically significant at a 0.10 level. That means that the number of matches does not deviate enough from 50%, or that the data are just not convincing enough for us to be sure the 46.2% figure we got wasn't caused by simple randomness.

16.   There is only a 1-in-9 chance that we could have gotten this result from a "random-walk" market.

17.   This is statistically significant at the 0.0001 level. There is a much less than 1-in-10,000 chance that these daily market returns came from a random walk.

18.   For technical reasons, we actually expect slightly more than 50% to be MATCHES. The mathematical expectation works out to under 50.1% for daily, monthly, and biennial MATCHES; 50.2% for quarterly; and just under 51% for annual MATCHES.

19.   In Myers & Miller, p. 511.

20.   This boils down to an argument about *market efficiency.* Overreaction and mean reversion do not prove that the market is inefficient. It might be true that investors require or deserve higher returns when prices are low, because stock returns generally exhibit more risk when price levels are low, and expected returns may be thought to be linked directly to expected risk. This is an important but complex technical point that is hotly debated among finance experts.

21.   By *growth-equalized*, I mean that the level of investment in the dollar cost and value averaging strategies is continually increased over time by the amount required to give the same basic overall market exposure. This is discussed in previous chapters.

22. You may be interested in how the dollar cost averaging strategy fares across various investment frequencies. You can see that its performance (relative to a constant share purchase) is not terribly sensitive to the investment frequency in the shorter-term "overreaction" zones, but degrades a bit using longer-term, mean-reverting frequencies. This reduced sensitivity makes sense, in that there is no selling under DCA strategies.

Details: 10
Getting Started

USING MUTUAL FUNDS

Throughout this book, most discussion and examples have assumed you are using some type of mutual fund for your investment program. The last sections of Chapters 1–3 pointed out some basic reasons why this is recommended. This section reviews your options, and it suggests that you consider using fully diversified low-expense no-load funds to carry out your formula strategy economically and effectively.

The Fund versus Stock Choice

If you are going to invest in the stock market, you could do so directly by buying shares of individual stocks, or you could indirectly buy the market by investing in mutual funds. There are two main reasons why you should use the indirect approach in implementing your formula plan: to minimize transaction costs (return enhancement) and to facilitate diversification (risk reduction).

Depending on which mutual fund you are considering and your volume of investing, your expenses for a formula plan can be much lower with a mutual fund. When you accumulate shares over time, low volume can cause sizable expenses with individual stocks but hardly any problem with most mutual funds. Small share purchases through a broker literally cost a fortune in terms of percentage of the amount invested. Some stocks provide dividend reinvestment plans and optional stock purchase plans directly through the company,[1] at no commision —perhaps one of the few routes for the individual investor to use low-cost DCA investing in individual stocks. There's really no sensible way to use value averaging with an individual stock, though. No-load mutual funds that have low numbers for turnover, management fees, and other expenses will do a much better job of keeping your investment expenses down to a reasonable minimum.

Perhaps more important than the expenses incurred with buying individual stocks over time is the unnecessary risk you take in your formula strategy. Using a single stock for dollar cost averaging would leave you so undiversified that the risk factor in your investment returns could double, or worse. Individual stocks have more volatile returns, can take extended moves in the wrong direction, and can even go bankrupt. After decades of dollar cost averaging in stocks in the buggy-whip industry, some investors ended up with nothing to show for their trouble. Even though diversified mutual funds do have uncertain returns that can go down for a while, they are not likely to head south and never return. Individual stocks have gone bankrupt, but the stock market as a whole has never done so (although it came close in the 1930s). This point is exceptionally important for the value averaging strategy, which involves such heavy buying on downturns (you certainly wouldn't want to "average" yourself all the way down to zero). It is critical that an investor using any variation of value averaging select an investment vehicle[2] that will not trend downward over extended time periods, such as a very diversified no-load mutual fund. You might even consider expanding your view of "the market," investing in one of the many funds that balances investments across a more diversified set of assets than just common stock.

No matter what fund you choose, most likely you will desire it to be "linked" with a money market mutual fund for simplified transfer of funds (telephone switching) into and out of your investment plan. Most stock funds have an associated money market fund or are a member of a broader "family of funds," giving you greater flexibility.

The mechanics are simple for using the fund in a value averaging plan. Once each month, quarter, or whatever period you choose, figure out how much you need to invest (or sell) to get the right value of your holdings. Ask yourself:

- What should the value of my holdings be this period? (Check your *value path.*)
- What is the actual current value of my holdings?
- What is the difference, which I must buy (or sell)?

Then call and make the transfer. Don't fret that the price you used for your calculation was yesterday's (today's price is yet unknown)—this minor uncertainty makes the VA process less exact but reduces the rate-of-return advantage over dollar cost averaging only by a negligible amount.

Index Funds

Although hundreds of mutual funds exist that are extremely well diversified, some have sales loads or very high expenses. If you feel that the value provided is worth the money, then no one has the right to keep you from buying into "expensive" mutual funds. But for all of the work that goes into trying to make each mutual fund outperform the stock market, the overwhelming evidence is that the vast majority of actively managed funds actually underperform the market. If you happen to know up front which funds will perform the best, then you certainly have better things to do with your time (and your substantial millions) than reading this book. If, however, like most of us you have no idea which funds will do best in the future, then there are several roads you can take to seek a fair return for your risk. Beyond picking a comfortable risk level, getting convenient services, and meeting a few other criteria, perhaps the most tangible thing you can do to help increase your net returns using mutual funds is to keep expenses as low as possible. *Stock index funds* generally fit this bill, as they strive merely to match some market index—not a bad goal in that doing so would put them well into the upper half (of long-run returns) of all mutual funds' performance. Due to the need for fewer active managers and less stock turnover, most index funds can provide diversified investment services with very low management fees and expense ratios. Thus, you can come very close to achieving the type of market returns seen in Chapter 1, without spending a lot on sales loads, management fees, and other expenses.

Information on Specific Funds

Remember, this book is not about mutual fund selection. Pick the mutual fund (or other investment vehicle) you are most comfortable with for use in your accumulation plan. Consistent with the discussion in the previous section, though, a few index funds and other mutual funds with very low expense ratios are provided in Table 10-1. In no way are the funds recommended as the best available, nor is the list exhaustive. It is merely a starting point to give you some basic information you may find helpful in your wider search for the right fund for you.

　　This list is by no means complete; there are certainly other perfectly good funds that were not listed[3]. Each fund here met several screening criteria[4] that made them potentially appropriate for use in a formula strategy such as value averaging. All of them require a low minimum investment (at least for an IRA), and they all have "telephone switch" privileges and an associated money market fund. They are all no-load funds, with an expense ratio of 1.0% of asset value or lower; the expense ratio (including management fee, 12b-1 charges, and the like) of these funds averages only 0.76%, about half of the equity fund average of 1.43%. They are very diversified funds, closely

TABLE 10-1 A Sampling of Equity Mutual Funds with Telephone Switching					
FUND NAME	Approx. Exp. Ratio	5-yr Annual Return	Risk[5]	Minimum Inv. Initial (IRA)/Subsequent	Phone
CGM Mutual Fund	0.97%	10.61%	Average	1000(250)/50	800/345-4048
Columbia Growth	0.96%	10.33	Average	1000(1000)/100	800/547-1707
Fidelity	0.66%	10.31	Low	2500(500)/250	800/544-8888
Financial Industrial	0.78%	8.90	High	250(250)/50	800/525-8085
Financial Ind. Income	0.76%	12.86	Low	250(250)/50	800/525-8085
Nicholas	0.82%	10.66	Average	500(500)/100	800/227-5987
State Farm Balanced	0.32%	13.63	VeryLow	50(50)/50	309/766-2029
State Farm Growth	0.25%	13.42	Average	50(50)/50	309/766-2029
Steinroe Stock	0.73%	9.86	High	1000(500)/100	800/338-2550
Twentieth Cent. Grth.	1.00%	11.75	VeryHigh	0(0)*/0	800/345-2021
Twentieth Cent. Sel.	1.00%	9.39	High	0(0)*/0	800/345-2021
Twentieth Cent. Ultra	1.00%	16.08	VeryHigh	0(0)*/0	800/345-2021
Value Line	0.71%	9.58	High	1000(1000)/100	800/223-0818
Value Line Lev. Grth.	0.97%	9.64	High	1000(1000)/100	800/223-0818
Van. Wld. Fd. US Grth.	0.74%	10.02	High	3000(500)/100	800/662-7447
Vanguard/Morgan	0.55%	10.90	Average	3000(500)/100	800/662-7447
Wm. Blair-Grth Shares	0.87%	9.17	Average	1000(1000)/250	800/635-2886
Vanguard Windsor II	0.52%	10.20	Average	3000(500)/100	800/662-7447

*An annual fee of $10 is charged to accounts under $1000

matching either the performance of the S&P 500 stock index or the NASDAQ average, for funds of smaller stocks. Using a standard measure of diversification[6], these funds are 91% diversified, compared with the average equity fund diversification of only 76% (100% is perfectly matching the index). In terms of the standard deviation of their returns, the average fund listed in Table 10-1 is slightly riskier than the average equity fund. The average annualized returns over the past 10 years favor the group above: 14.2% annual return (281% total return) versus the equity fund average of 12.6% annually (239% total). Numbers for the five-year average are 11.0% compared to the average fund's 8.5%; for the shorter three-year period this group returned an average 15.2% versus the overall average of 9.9%. These may not be all the best funds for you to consider, but they are certainly not a bad lot to choose from for an affordable, well-diversified equity investment. Don't just pick the fund with the highest historical return—it varies by the period chosen, and past performance is no real indicator of future success. Look at all the variables that concern you.

For investors who hold other assets besides just the one mutual fund, another relevant measure of risk is *beta,* a number that simply measures the amount of "co-movement" with the market. The average stock would have a beta of 1. If a stock has a beta of 0.6 and the market moved up 10% over a very short period, you would expect (on average) a 6% gain on the stock.[7] The basic intuition is that high-beta stocks are riskier, even after you diversify them by putting them in a portfolio with other stocks. As a result, we expect that stocks (funds) with a higher beta will achieve a higher investment return, on average (deeper intuition about beta is beyond the scope of this book). The average equity mutual fund has a beta of 0.6–0.7 (depending on how/when you measure it), in that many hold a lot of cash, bonds, and other low-risk items as well as stock. In Table 10-1, the very low-risk funds have a beta of 0.5–0.6; the low-risk funds, 0.7–0.8; the average funds, 0.8–0.9; high-risk at 1.0–1.1; and the very high-risk funds have a beta of 1.1–1.3. The beta risk measure will help you (later in this chapter) with determining a reasonable estimate for the expected return factor *r*. Most of the major sources of mutual fund information available in libraries include an estimate of each fund's beta.[8]

There are a few other promising funds for your potential use, but they do not allow telephone switching, which may not be a concern to many investors. Here are four that may meet your needs:

- *Dodge & Cox Stock Fund* has only a 0.65% expense ratio and a 97% diversification, almost as good as an index fund. Their 5- and 10-year average returns are 11.9% and 16.1%. Its beta, like the beta of the Vanguard index funds below, is just under 1.00. Phone (415) 434-0311.
- *Dodge & Cox Balanced Fund* is a very low-risk option with a low 0.63 beta. It has a 0.70% expense ratio, 96% diversification, and 5- and 10-year average returns of 11.0% and 14.6%.
- *Vanguard Index Trust 500* is an index fund, with an incredible 0.22% expense ratio and a 100% diversification (it matches the index). The 5- and 10-year average returns are 11.6% and 15.1%. Phone (800) 662-7447.
- *Vanguard Quantitative Portfolio* is a similar but newer fund, but uses a little fancy footwork with more active management to try to eke out more return than the index fund. The expense ratio is 0.64%, the diversification is 99%, and it has an above-average 3-year return of 14.3%.

In choosing a fund, remember that low cost, diversification, reasonable performance, and convenience are all factors that should weigh heavily if you plan on using the fund profitably in a long-term formula investment plan (or even if you're just going to "buy and hold").

WORKING OUT THE DETAILS

As you've no doubt noticed by now, a multitude of sensible options are available for implementing a DCA or VA formula plan. This section tries to address some of the more common questions and concerns about putting a plan into action, while giving pointers on how to tailor one that fits your needs. Even though working out all the details ahead of time is an admirable goal, you should avoid becoming so paralyzed by details that you forget to start investing. As you gain experience with trying out different variations to the basic strategies, much of what you do will be "made up as you go along." That's OK, as long as you remember not to chicken out at market bottoms or get too excited at market peaks. A major goal of these formula strategies is to provide a discipline to guide you through these extremely emotional times in the market, sometimes against your "better judgment" (which judgment after the fact seldom turns out to have been better).

Examples of planning and executing these strategies, with all of their "real-life" complications, are provided in Chapter 11.

Using a Side Fund

With value averaging, or any other formula plan that involves purchases and sales, you should have a side fund in addition to your main investment fund. The obvious choice for this is a money market fund in the same family of funds as the primary fund in which you are investing.

The sometimes radical cash flows resulting from value averaging strategy scare some people at first glance. For example, after the October 1987 crash, you would have needed to invest a huge sum to meet your value goal the next month. Where would it have come from? From the *other half* of the value averaging—from previous sales. As the market went a little crazy going up in early 1987, you would have been selling a lot of "excess" shares to meet your value goal. You aren't supposed to take this money out and have a huge party with it. You should put it in the side fund until it is needed back in the market after a later market dip—post-October 1987, for example. You won't always have money in the side fund, though, particularly when the market is down. After all, this is not a self-financing strategy that creates value out of thin air.

One problem with value averaging is that you can't automatically have the "right amount" transferred from your checking account into your investment fund every month (or other period). But if you establish a side fund that has telephone exchange privileges into your investment fund, you can set up an automatic investment using the following procedure. Start out with a little "buffer" money in the side fund—you may need it if the market goes down, and you have to have an initial investment anyway to start up in a money market fund. Next, set up an automatic transfer on a periodic (usually monthly) basis from your checking account into your money market (side) fund. The fixed amount you set up should be roughly equal to the value of $C (as described in Chapter 5), the effective net monthly investment in value averaging that was similar to the monthly amount in dollar cost averaging. Over time (every year or two), you should adjust this fixed amount up (increase $C at rate g, as discussed in Chapters 4 and 5) to keep up with increased prices. Then, each month or quarter (or period of your choice for "doing" value averaging), calculate your required investment, and make a telephone transfer of that amount from the side fund into your main investment fund. When a sale of shares is called for and you go through with it, just transfer the proceeds into your side fund, where you'll keep them for a rainy day. Always maintain a side fund with value averaging if you plan to sell shares. You may need the money later when the plan calls for a sizable investment (after prices drop); if not, then you get an unexpected "bonus" return.

Operating Within a Retirement Account

Due to the tax advantages, a retirement account (IRA, Keogh, or SEP, for example) is the obvious place to implement a strategy such as value averaging. Because taxes are deferred in such plans, the fact that value averaging involves selling has no downside, as your gains taxes would be deferred. But because you can't, as a rule, take money out of your retirement account at will, you need to establish a side fund along with your investment fund to hold your "winnings."

Suppose you decide to use value averaging within an IRA, and you want to invest the full $2,000 each year. You can send $166.66 ($2,000 divided by 12 months) into the money market fund portion of the IRA using an automatic transfer. Then every period on your value path, call up and transfer the required money into or out of your stock mutual fund, also in the same IRA. Just make sure you set a value path that is reasonably small, considering your $166.66 monthly IRA investment limitation. You wouldn't want to start with a value of $C that was already high, like $150. If you start out a value path that is too high, you may end with a recommended amount to buy that exceeds the amount you have in your IRA side fund, if the market goes down. Obviously you shouldn't exceed the investment limits of your IRA, so you would just temporarily fall short of your value goal if the market did that poorly.

If your future goals are sizable, they may dictate a value path that demands sizable purchases, perhaps much more than the $2,000 per year allowed into your IRA account. You could meet your goals, though, by investing in a *non*-IRA account once you hit your $2,000 annual limit. More on this at the end of this chapter.

Establishing a Value Path

Chapters 4 and 5 went into great length about how to calculate the required investments and value path for the strategies over time. There are lots of options in this process, so it pays to be reasonable and make decisions now that you know you can live with later. A few guidelines in this section help you establish the value path (for value averaging) or the required investments (for dollar cost averaging) for your plan.

Recall that there are four pieces of information you need to help complete your investment puzzle. First is your final target or goal—$V accumulated in t years. The other three inputs are $C (your initial investment quantity for the first period); r, the expected rate of return on your investment; and g, the amount by which you are willing to increase your periodic investment ($C) each period. You must determine your own investment goal (remember to allow for the effects of inflation!), and you likely have some good concept of how much ($C) you can contribute right now toward that goal each period. We'll spend a bit of time now on the other two inputs: the growth factors r and g.

Remember, the process is not exact—you really don't know what the market will do in the future. To that end, be a little conservative in your assumptions about market growth—conservative, but not timid. With government bond rates in the 7–8% range, a monthly r of about 1.0% for the expected rate of return on the stock market is reasonably conservative. Table 10-2 provides representative figures to use for r, the expected rate of return on your fund investment. If you invest quarterly and use quarterly figures in the formulas (from Chapter 4 or 5), then use the top of Table 10-2. If you invest monthly, you want to use the monthly rates of return in the bottom half of the table. Using a method[9] similar to the calculation of the expected return on the stock market in Chapter 1, the expected return on a fund investment is calculated based on the interest rate and the fund's beta measure of risk. For example, if the 10-year Treasury bond rate is 8.0% and you have a fund with slightly below-average market risk (ß = 0.9), use a monthly r of 1.01% or a quarterly r of 3.0% in any formulas that project compound growth or value paths over time. If you want to be conservative, then round the interest rate and the beta measure *down* to the lower cell.

TABLE 10-2 Expected Compound[10] Return—*Quarterly* (Use the number in the table as figure for quarterly *r*)						
10-Yr Bond Rate	Beta of the Mutual Fund					
	0.7	0.8	0.9	1.0	1.1	1.2
6.0%	2.3%	2.4%	2.6%	2.7%	2.9%	3.0%
7.0%	2.5%	2.7%	2.8%	3.0%	3.1%	3.2%
7.5%	2.7%	2.8%	2.9%	3.1%	3.2%	3.4%
8.0%	2.8%	2.9%	3.0%	3.2%	3.3%	3.5%
8.5%	2.9%	3.0%	3.2%	3.3%	3.4%	3.6%
9.0%	3.0%	3.1%	3.3%	3.4%	3.6%	3.7%
10%	3.2%	3.4%	3.5%	3.6%	3.8%	3.9%
12%	3.7%	3.8%	4.0%	4.1%	4.2%	4.4%

USE THE **TOP** TABLE FOR **QUARTERLY** FIGURES;

USE THE **BOTTOM** TABLE FOR **MONTHLY** FIGURES

Expected Compound Return—*Monthly* (Use the number in the table as figure for monthly *r*)						
10-Yr Bond Rate	Beta of the Mutual Fund					
	0.7	0.8	0.9	1.0	1.1	1.2
6.0%	0.76%	0.81%	0.86%	0.90%	0.95%	1.00%
7.0%	0.84%	0.88%	0.93%	*0.98%*	1.02%	1.07%
7.5%	0.88%	0.92%	0.97%	1.01%	1.06%	1.11%
8.0%	0.91%	0.96%	1.01%	1.05%	1.10%	1.14%
8.5%	0.95%	1.00%	1.04%	1.09%	1.13%	1.18%
9.0%	0.99%	1.03%	1.08%	1.13%	1.17%	1.22%
10%	1.06%	1.11%	1.15%	1.20%	1.24%	1.29%

Use the top table to estimate the expected *quarterly* return "*r*," on your investment. Use the bottom table for the expected *monthly* return, "*r*." Round interest rates and fund betas down if you want to be conservative. *These numbers are on a before-tax basis and must be adjusted for taxes if you pay taxes on your gains each year.*

The *r* growth factor just discussed refers to the expected growth of money you have already invested. The other growth factor, *g,* refers not to investment results, but to increases in your own contributions to the investment fund. In dollar cost averaging, *g* is simply the amount by which your investment changes from month to month (or whatever period is used). In value averaging, *g* is the amount of increase in your *expected* contribution each period, on average (that is, if your fund grows in value at the expected return, *r*). If you want to keep your net investment amount a little ahead of inflation, a reasonable value for *g* is roughly the T-bond[11] rate (on an annual basis—divide it by 4 or 12 to get an approximate value to use for quarterly or monthly investing). You could also use the same value for *g* as you did for *r*; however, your required investment contribution would grow at a very steep rate over time. The lower you peg *r* and *g*, the less chance there is that you'll be unpleasantly surprised by failing to meet your investment goal, or by having to shell out higher-than-planned amounts to invest.

Setting Up a VA Value Path: An Example

Here's an example of how to set up a value path for a value averaging strategy.

Fred and Kathy Smith are considering a monthly value averaging plan. Recall that formula **(19)** from Chapter 5 for the value averaging value path was:

$$V_t = C \times t \times (1+R)^t \quad \text{where } R = \frac{r+g}{2}$$

The Smiths plan to send their eight-year-old daughter to a public college in 10 years. Based on a recent Education Department study and their own calculations, the Smiths expect the average annual cost of a public college to be $12,500 by the 2001–02 school year. If a fund of $50,000 is accumulated in 10 years, it should be sufficient; interest after that point should keep up with the increases in later tuition years. They will use 20th Century Select Fund, which has a beta of about 1.07; the current T-bond rates are around 7.2%. Using Table 10-2, the pretax value to use for r is seen to be 0.98% monthly—that's the expected rate of return over the average month for their fund investments. This fund is actively managed, so almost all of the capital gains are paid out and taxed each year, along with the fairly sizable dividends. Still, some of the gains accrue tax-deferred, and the Smiths estimate that their effective tax rate (they are in the 28% tax bracket) on fund investment returns is about 24%. Still, to be conservative, they use the full 28% tax rate here; that means that the after-tax rate of return is not 0.98% but only 72% (100% - 28%) of that, or 0.7%. The Smiths also expect to increase their average expected monthly contribution to the fund at roughly the T-bond rate of 7.2% annually, or 7.2% ÷ 12 or 0.6% monthly. Thus, the growth factors they will use are:

$$r_{after\ tax} = 0.7\% \qquad g = 0.6\% \qquad R = 0.65\% = 0.0065$$

Recall that R is just the average of the two growth factors. Now they can solve for $C, in the formula:

$$\$50,000 = \$C \times 120 \times (1.0065)^{120}$$

$$\$C = \$191.49$$

So the value path for month t with value averaging would then be:

$$V_t = \$191.49 \times t \times (1.0065)^t$$

The Smiths could establish $t = 0$ as right now, and no investment would be due yet ($V_0 = 0$). Next month, the value path is $192.73, so in a month they would have to invest that amount. They would invest enough two months from now to increase their fund holdings to meet the value path of $387.97;

in a year, $2,484; and after 10 years, the goal of $50,000. You could always establish $t = 0$ as the previous month, so that it is $t = 1$ right now, and you can start investing right away (and achieve your goal a month quicker).

Alternative #1. If the Smiths wanted to use a higher investment amount, $200 for example, and set $t = 0$ at the previous month, so that $t = 1$ now and $t = 121$ in 10 years, they could instead calculate a value path by solving for R instead of C:

$$\$50,000 = 200 \times 121 \times (1+R)^{121}$$

which yields a value of $R = 0.0060$, or $R = 0.60\%$. Because R is the average of the 0.70% after-tax expected rate of return r and the contribution growth factor g, then g must be 0.50% for the average to work out to 0.60%. This g is a (roughly) 6% annual increase in their expected investment contribution. Using $R = 0.0060$, the value path they should follow is:

$$V_t = \$200 \times t \times (1.0060)^t$$

and if $t = 1$ right now, their first investment should be for $201.20.

Alternative #2. The Smiths think they can increase their contributions over time at a faster rate than the $g = 0.50\%$ that was (implicitly) used in the last value path. Suppose they wanted to stay with the $g = 0.60\%$ (derived from the T-bond rate) used in the first example, giving the original average growth factor of $R = 0.65\%$. Putting this, with $C = 200$, back into the value path formula, they could just use the formula:

$$V_t = \$200 \times t \times (1.0065)^t$$

With the $t = 1$ timing just discussed, in 10 years ($t = 121$), the resulting value is calculated to be $53,000, or $3,000 over their goal. This alternative is actually quite conservative, in that the plan to overshoot the goal yields a $3,000 future "buffer" in case anything goes wrong.

The Smith example has provided various methods of initial planning for the use of value averaging to achieve your investment goal. A much more complete example is presented in the next chapter.

Other Important Considerations

It is important to *readjust* your plan from time to time. One of the few universal truths in financial markets is that things change. No matter which strategy you use, you must reevaluate it every year or so to see if you are still on track with your ultimate investment goal, given your portfolio's performance and any changes in the investment environment.

One simple but often overlooked step in setting ultimate investment goals is to consider inflation. If typical college costs are $60,000 today, it would be unrealistic to use $60,000 as your investment goal for your newborn's college fund. Take a reasonable guess as to what that goal needs to be *in the future*, inflation and all. It's OK if you gradually find you were wrong, because you should continually readjust your investment plan to account for miscalculations and new information.

Don't feel you must follow the plan to the penny. If you are dollar cost averaging and your plan is to increase your monthly investment amount at a 0.5% monthly rate (a bit over 6% annually), you probably wouldn't want to go to the trouble of actually increasing your investment every month—you more likely would automatically transfer the same amount each month. Simply adjust it each year. Start with an investment 3% higher; if you planned an initial amount of $100, invest $103 instead. As the required investment grows monthly on paper at a 6% annual rate (to $106), you will be 3% *behind* by the end of the year. So on average, it balances out to about the right amount over the entire year. Then at the end of the year, get back to 3% over your required amount (to about $109) by increasing your first-year amount by the necessary 6% or so. This approach is a lot easier, and it should preserve your sanity.

Finally, don't forget that the relatively risky investments in your formula plans should be only a portion of your overall portfolio. Very few investors would be well served by having their entire portfolio of wealth all rolled up in a single asset.

Using Guidelines and Limits

You should establish sensible guidelines and limits for your investment plan so you can feel truly comfortable with it. We have already covered several such guidelines in previouis chapters. For example, if you find yourself only a few dollars away from your value path, there's really no need to buy 0.013 shares to equate to exactly the right value. Small variances like this will be picked up during the next period. Another example of such a guideline is the no-sell variation of value averaging, which may be better for some people in some situations (see Chapter 6). Another variation of this that has some nice properties discussed earlier (see Chapter 6 and 9) is to *delay* sales for a month or two.

One important guideline to determine up front is how often you will value average. Whereas most examples in this book have used a monthly period, a quarterly period may be better from a return standpoint, and in terms of lowering transaction costs and saving time. Using automatic monthly investments into a side fund and then doing value averaging on a less-frequent basis was mentioned earlier in this chapter.

One of the key concerns of some investors with the value averaging strategy is the perceived danger (as opposed to *opportunity*) of the larger share purchases after market dips—imagine the size of the "required investment" after the 1987 crash. If that concerns you, you can limit the volatility of the cash flow in several ways. Let's say you have a value averaging plan that currently involves roughly a $100 monthly increase. You could limit your monthly purchase to no greater than *some* amount, such as $300, $500, or $1,000—whatever maximum you're comfortable with. Remember that much of this money probably came from prior sales of shares in the strategy, so the large sums being "invested" really aren't always new contributions you had to scrape up. Taking this idea a step further, you could limit new contributions only. That is, you could invest any amount—as long as your side fund covers it—but never more than, say, $200 of "new money." There are many ways to craft your own limits now to avoid excessive responses and guide your actions in later turbulent times. Well-thought-out guidelines may protect you against straying from your plan in a desire to follow the crowd.

It's *your* investment program and it's your money. Make sure that the plan you follow is one you can be comfortable with, especially when times are particularly good or bad.

NOTES FOR FINANCIAL PLANNERS

Because some investors shy away from calculators and figures in general, financial planners often may find themselves dealing with some sort of formula plan as part of their advisory duties.[12] This section briefly highlights a few points concerning these plans that may be of interest to planners.

The guidelines and limits outlined above should be thought about by the financial planner, and discussed and perhaps "paper-traded" with the investor prior to any agreement to implement a plan. In familiarizing the investor with the process, the planner should lay out the value path and expected increase in the amount invested, as well as the projected portfolio value over time. Along the same lines, the planner should ensure that the investor understands the crucial role of the side fund as part of the investment plan in value averaging. The investor must *not* think of the side fund as a pot of bonus money to be spent immediately.

Dealing with inflation and taxes provides an opportunity for the financial planner to truly add value to this process. Reasoned input is important here, not only to make decent estimates of the ultimate investment value goal, but to evaluate how investor contributions might increase over time. The planner should integrate the long-term budget with information about expected changes in the availability of investment money. Perhaps investment accumulation can be programmed to accelerate now while income is increasing and demands are low so that later, when the family's needs are greater, growth can be slowed. The plan should also be sensibly integrated into the overall investment portfolio; that is, limits should be established so that investment mixes don't get too far out of whack, and so that the entire bond portion of the portfolio won't need to be sold to buy into the value averaging fund after the stock market turns down.

Because reassessing performance and readjusting the plan is a possible area of planner involvement, financial planners should master the material in Chapters 4 and 5. Investment amounts, portfolio values, and value paths should be analyzed every year or so to ensure that the trajectory of the investment plan is still going to carry the investor to a pot of the required size at the end of the rainbow. Any change in an investor's situation may require readjustment of the parameters of an established plan. Good examples of handling these and other complications are provided in Chapter 11.

Advanced Methods

Planners and investors may want to consider a few "advanced" possibilities.

It may be wise, and fairly simple, to take advantage of the term structure of interest rates instead of putting the VA side fund only into a money market fund. As of this writing, money-market interest rates are a few percentage points below the rates of CDs and intermediate-term bonds. For instance, if a bull market has your side fund flush with cash and your guidelines limit how quickly it can end up reinvested back into the main fund, then you can squeeze a little more yield out of the side fund by taking advantage of an upward-sloping term structure with bank CDs or a short-term bond fund. This may be more trouble than it is worth but would be beneficial in certain situations.

Another option with any of these strategies is to use closed-end mutual funds as the investment vehicle. Because closed-end funds are traded in the marketplace and involve commissions, this would probably make sense only for substantial investment plans. Still, many investors like closed-end funds for their discount feature. For the motivated and experienced investor, there are several well-diversified, closed-end funds available at a "discount" that might be viable for a formula plan. The investment amount could even be adjusted for the size of the discount, relative to some historical norm such as a 200-week moving average. However, I wouldn't recommend this option if the commissions involved would be at all significant relative to the size of the investment.[13]

A final point of interest to planners has to do with using a *split investment fund,* best explained with an example. If you're using value averaging as part of your IRA and one month you need to invest more than the tax laws allow, there's nothing stopping you from investing the required amount *outside* your IRA, into a taxable account. Your value averaging investment would now be *split* between two funds. Later, if a sale was dictated, you would sell some of the IRA shares (moving the proceeds to the IRA side fund)—not the taxable shares—thus avoiding any tax liability. The split-fund approach has other applications to reduce transaction costs. For example, if you were to invest in closed-end funds, you would hate to sell and incur another brokerage commission. But if you split your investment between a normal fund and a closed-end fund, you could make all required sales out of the normal fund, thus avoiding excessive brokerage charges. Many investment programs could benefit from splitting funds between a base fund and a transaction fund, using the latter to effect transactions more cost effectively.

SUMMARY

There are limitless variations you could employ in executing a formula strategy. While previous chapters discussed the pro's and con's of many of these variations, this chapter focused on employing them in a manner that you are *comfortable* with. Your decisions and actions alone will determine whether your investment plan gets results you can live with in good times and bad. So, tailor a plan you can be happy with!

ENDNOTES

1.   Nearly all of the companies require that you be a shareholder before enrolling you in these purchase plans. To get your first share, there are three organizations that I know of that provide an alternative to using a broker. For a nominal service charge, they can arrange for the purchase of one share in many of the companies that offer dividend reinvestment and stock purchase plans. They are:

First Share, Marti Mernitz and Associates, 28 East 55th St., Indianapolis, IN 46220. (800) 683-0743.
Moneypaper, (a newsletter—Vita Nelson, editor), 1010 Mamaroneck Ave., Mamaroneck, NY 10543. (914) 381-5400.
National Association of Investors Corporation, 1515 East Eleven Mile Road, Royal Oak, MI 48067. (313) 543-0612.

2.   In view of this discussion, I suppose it's possible to value average a portfolio of individual stocks through a dividend reinvestment/ optional stock purchase plan; but, you would have to be careful. Suppose you had two stocks (you ought to have more!), and you used DCA to invest $200 in stock ABC and $100 in stock XYZ, monthly. If you wanted to value average your purchases, you should *not* set up separate value paths and use VA with each stock separately. You could, though, apply VA *techniques* to the *total* (portfolio) value, and

then divide the portfolio investment between the stocks. For example, you could set value targets of $300 (Month 1) and $600 (Month 2) for your two-stock portfolio. If, at Month 2, your ABC had gone down to $170, and XYZ to $70 (for a $240 total), VA would call for a $360 investment. You would divide this: $240 to ABC and $120 to XYZ. Also, as selling is cumbersome in these programs, you would likely use the "no-sell" variation described in Chapter 6.

3.   The previous edition listed several funds not shown here. These are good funds that didn't quite meet all the screening criteria; the selection process is fairly sensitive to the time period chosen. The other funds are: Fidelity Trend, Founders Blue Chip, Janus, SAFECO Equity, SAFECO Growth, Steinroe Special, Vanguard Star, and Wellington.

4.   The data analysis comes from the Rugg & Steele data base, which is also used by *Kiplinger's Personal Finance* and other magazines in constructing their annual mutual fund articles. All data were current as of June 1991.

5.   Risk is measured relative to the market index, or the S&P 500 stock index in this case. Average risk is about 2.0% (weekly return standard deviation). The "Very High" and "Very Low" risk funds varied from the average by more than 25%.

6.   The correlation coefficient (with the S&P 500 index) is given, put into percent form for exposition. Perfect diversification relative to the S&P index would give a coefficient of 1.00—in fact, a few index funds report a 0.99 or higher. The average correlation coefficient relative to the NASDAQ index for this group of funds was 0.87, compared with the average equity fund coefficient of 0.75. In this group, the highest "large stock" correlations (with the S&P 500) were 0.96, for 20th Century Select, Windsor II, and Vanguard Morgan. The highest "small stock" correlations (with NASDAQ) were .91-.92, for Nicholas, Columbia Growth, and Value Line Leveraged Growth.

7.   Actually, these are "excess returns" as compared to sure-thing returns—gain over and above riskless government interest rates. So, if interest rates are 8% and the market gains 18% (a 10% "excess"), a stock with a 0.6 beta would expect (on average) a 6% "excess" over the interest rate, or a 14% gain.

8.   On such source is *The Individual Investor's Guide to No-Load Mutual Funds*, 12 ed. (Chicago: International Publishing Corporation, 1993).

9.   There are a few differences in this more complex calculation. The simple return over and above the interest rate, called the *risk premium*, depends on the value of beta (it is beta × market risk premium). Then there is an adjustment to convert the average of the variable returns into what the compound return would be if it were smooth (nonvariable). This is an arithmetic-to-geometric mean converstion, necessary because the formula assumes the same rate compounded (geometrically) over many periods. The formulas involved are beyond the scop of this book.

10.   The "Expected Compound Return" is the *geometric* average expected, which is smaller than the common (arithmetic) average expected return. This applies to calculations where the varying returns will be compounded over time, as in the formulas for DCA targets and VA value paths.

11.   Use any long-term T-bond rate, such as the 10-year rate used in Table 10-2. The short-term T-bill rate is too unstable for use in the long-term formulas.

12.   Since its introduction, many financial planners have been using value averaging successfully with clients in their practice.

13.   For more information on closed-end funds, see Frank Cappiello, *The Complete Guide to Closed-End Funds: Finding Value in Today's Stock Market,* 5th Ed. Chicago: International Publishing Corporation, 1993.

Examples:
Strategies at Work 11

The previous chapter discussed several of the details and strategy twists you might want to consider in tailoring and using your own investment strategy for accumulating wealth. To really apply the seemingly basic accumulation strategies, you must determine your goal, choose an investment, estimate market return and investment growth figures, establish a value path (for VA), and then implement your plan to achieve your goal. Throughout the process, you must deal with the changes and realities of the marketplace—you should reevaluate your goal (as inflation changes), your progress toward that goal (as your investment returns vary), and the risk you are willing to bear (as you get closer to your goal). This chapter shows you how to put all this together and how to keep it together over time.

While I hope each of many previous hints and tips made sense in isolation, I suspect they are easier to digest if actually seen in action. How would a real investor put the DCA or VA strategies to work in real life, facing the real taxes, uncertainties, and other complications that we invariably must deal with over time?

We'll look at thorough examples of putting the DCA and VA strategies to work. We'll follow a mutual fund investor through a 10-year period (ending in 1991) of accumulation in a real investment, the *Vanguard Index Trust 500* mutual fund. We'll see how to deal with realities like inflation, taxes, and market variability, and how to keep our investment target in our sights by monitoring and readjusting our position as needed. The chapter is very detail oriented, very reality oriented, so you can hopefully see how to apply the lessons learned in prior chapters.

THE GOAL AND INVESTMENT ENVIRONMENT

The time is December 31, 1981. Larry wants some land to build a vacation cabin. Nothing fancy, just a spot in the hills near a lake in a nearby state. Larry doesn't yet have anything saved up for his dream, but would like to be able to buy the land outright in ten years (and would then be able to finance the cabin). His typical dream lot costs just under $58,000 right now, and he expects these land prices to stay even with inflation over time.

Choosing an Investment

Larry could choose to meet his goal by investing in fixed income securities (bonds, CDs, etc.) that would exactly meet his goal in ten years (December 1991) with very little risk—if he had the money now to invest. Even in that case, such a plan would not work out very well, for at least two reasons. First of all, the future price of the lot will vary with future inflation, which is uncertain, and makes fixed income investments a poor fit. Second, the return on fixed income is quite low.

Equity investments help with both of these problems to some extent. Since he has no money saved yet, Larry will need to accumulate wealth toward that goal over the next ten years. Larry wants a no-load, low-expense, well diversified equity investment, and chooses the *Vanguard Index Trust 500* mutual fund (which is described following Table 10-1 in Chapter 10). We will use actual price and dividend data provided by that fund for the period December 31, 1981 – December 31, 1991. This will turn out to be a very good investment for Larry (the fund averages over 17% annually over the coming 10 years); of course, he can't possibly know this back in 1981.

Continued on page 197.

TABLE 11-1: Quarterly Price and Return Data for *Vanguard Index Trust 500* Mutual Fund				
Quarter	Price (N.A.V.)	Distribution	Total Return	$1 in 1981 becomes
Dec 81	$15.52			$1.00
Mar 82	$14.23	$.01157	-7.16%	$0.93
Jun 82	$13.99	$.01259	-0.43%	$0.92
Sep 82	$15.36	$.01257	11.05%	$1.03
Dec 82	$17.56	$.03512	17.83%	$1.21
Mar 83	$19.08	$.01034	9.69%	$1.33
Jun 83	$20.93	$.00957	10.65%	$1.47
Sep 83	$20.70	$.00851	-0.25%	$1.46
Dec 83	$19.70	$.05011	0.18%	$1.47
Mar 84	$19.08	$.00909	-2.24%	$1.43
Jun 84	$18.40	$.00945	-2.62%	$1.40
Sep 84	$19.98	$.00978	9.57%	$1.53
Dec 84	$19.52	$.04127	1.83%	$1.56
Mar 85	$21.11	$.00928	9.07%	$1.70
Jun 85	$22.46	$.00852	7.25%	$1.82
Sep 85	$21.38	$.00801	-4.01%	$1.75
Dec 85	$22.99	$.09334	16.86%	$2.05
Mar 86	$26.02	$.00783	13.96%	$2.33
Jun 86	$27.34	$.00695	5.77%	$2.47
Sep 86	$25.21	$.00658	-7.13%	$2.29
Dec 86	$24.27	$.09197	5.47%	$2.41

	TABLE 11-1: Quarterly Price and Return Data for *Vanguard Index Trust 500* Mutual Fund *(cont.)*			
Quarter	Price (N.A.V.)	Distribution	Total Return	$1 in 1981 becomes
Mar 87	$29.23	$.00731	21.17%	$2.93
Jun 87	$30.52	$.00608	5.02%	$3.07
Sep 87	$32.31	$.00590	6.45%	$3.27
Dec 87	$24.65	$.01001	-22.71%	$2.53
Mar 88	$25.67	$.01505	5.64%	$2.67
Jun 88	$27.15	$.00704	6.47%	$2.84
Sep 88	$27.06	$.00670	0.34%	$2.85
Dec 88	$27.18	$.02535	2.98%	$2.94
Mar 89	$28.74	$.01299	7.04%	$3.14
Jun 89	$31.09	$.00611	8.79%	$3.42
Sep 89	$34.20	$.00580	10.58%	$3.78
Dec 89	$33.64	$.03654	2.02%	$3.86
Mar 90	$32.38	$.00680	-3.07%	$3,74
Jun 90	$34.21	$.00560	6.21%	$3.97
Sep 90	$29.32	$.00535	-13.76%	$3.43
Dec 90	$31.24	$.02333	8.88%	$3.73
Mar 91	$35.51	$.00800	14.47%	$4.27
Jun 91	$35.23	$.00503	-0.29%	$4.26
Sep 91	$36.91	$.00513	5.28%	$4.48
Dec 91	$39.31	$.01840	8.34%	$4.86
Average Annualized Return: +17.12%				

Setting the Goal (Dealing with Inflation)

How much money will Larry need for his goal? $58,000? Only if he can make time (or the price level) stand still. If the 1981 price is about $58,000, then inflation will drive the future (1991) price well above that figure. At a 7% inflation rate, prices almost double in 10 years.

What expected inflation rate should Larry use? No one knows for sure. Inflation was pretty high back in 1981; high interest rates reflected people's expectations that high inflation would continue (we know *now* that it didn't, but that's with a decade of hindsight). Some of the relevant economic information from 1981 is shown in the top row of Table 11-2. The inflation rate had been 8.9% during 1981, and Treasury bills returned 14.7% that year. For 1982, Treasury bills prom-

TABLE 11-2 Relevant Rates, 1981-1991			
Year	Actual Inflation	US Treasury Bill Return	Int. Gov't Bond Yield
1981	8.9	14.7	14.0
1982	3.9	10.5	9.9
1983	3.8	8.8	11.4
1984	4.0	9.9	11.0
1985	3.8	7.7	8.6
1986	1.1	6.2	6.9
1987	4.4	5.5	8.3
1988	4.4	6.4	9.2
1989	4.7	8.4	7.9
1990	6.1	7.8	7.7
1991	3.1	5.6	6.0

ised (as of the end of 1981) to return 10.5%. Market yields on intermediate Treasury bond yields at the end of 1981 were 14.0%.

With this information, one can roughly approximate a reasonable estimate of the inflation rate to be expected in the future. It will seldom be very accurate, but on average, it is better than a good guess. One way to think about inflation in the future is that recent inflation rates give a good guide; by this approach, 8.9% would be the expected inflation rate. This approach ignores the important fact that the future is seldom like, or even expected to be like, the past. We can turn to Treasury bill and bond yields to get some idea of what the financial markets expect inflation to be in the future.

Yields on bills and bonds generally provide investors with an expected return *over and above* inflation. Long-term investments (bonds) historically provide, on average, almost a 1% higher excess return than do short-term investments like bills. In modern times, as a long-run average, bonds seem to provide about a 3% "bonus" over expected rates of inflation; short-term bills give about 2% above-inflation returns. Since Treasury bonds were yielding 14.0% at the end of 1981, a reasonable expectation of long-term future inflation rates would be 3% lower, or 11.0%. One-year Treasury bills were promising to return 10.5% over the next year (and did so); thus, based on these yields, an expected inflation rate over the next year would be 2% lower, or 8.5%.

Consolidating the various educated guesses about future inflation would give Larry about a 10% inflation estimate to use in the future. The old inflation rate (8.9%) and the expected next-year inflation rate (8.5%) may be fine for the immediate future, but they are flimsy indicators for our 10-year time frame. A better figure is the intermediate term (7-10 year) expected inflation estimate of 11.0%. Averaging the estimates, but giving more weight to the more relevant figure, gives us a 10% inflation estimate.

At a 10% annual inflation rate, $1 grows to $2.59 in price over 10 years. Thus, Larry's land, priced at nearly $58,000 currently, will cost him about $150,000 (= 58,000 × 2.59) in 1991. This is merely an estimate; if inflation settles below 10%, the land will cost less. But for now, Larry's investment goal, accounting for expected inflation, is **$150,000**.

How Much Should He Invest?

Accumulating $150,000 from a standing start in 10 years is quite a task. Ignoring interest, that's $1,250 per month, or $3,750 per quarter. The task is much less daunting, however, since Larry can expect a positive return on money he can invest.

Larry figures he can save about $400-$500 monthly at this time; although, he has no idea whether that will be enough (or too much) to meet his goal. A very simple approach is to use the annuity formula #4-4 (Chapter 4, formula 4) to see what a series of $400 regular monthly investments would grow to over 10 years. (For ease of reference, I've repeated the most important formulas in a box at the end of this chapter.) If we assume an average compound monthly return of 1% (12.68% annually), the account would grow to only $92,000.[1] A $500 monthly investment would accrue to $115,000 over 10 years.[2]

To keep his bookkeeping simpler, Larry decides he will invest quarterly, for 40 quarters. He can afford about $1,200 to $1,500 per quarter. Assuming an average compound quarterly return of 3% (12.55% annually), he could accumulate anywhere between $90,500 ($1,200 at the end of each quarter) and $116,500 ($1,500 at the start of each quarter). Using a financial calculator to compute the required investment as shown in Chapter 4, we find that Larry needs to set aside about $1,990/quarter for 40 quarters, and earn a compound average annual return of 12.55% *after taxes*, in order to meet his goal.[3] This is about $660 per month; is the goal beyond his reach? To answer this, let's examine the expected return on investment more closely, along with taxes, and then look at Larry's options.

INVESTMENT RETURN & TAXES

What return on investment should Larry project into the future? The higher the assumed return, the easier it will *appear* for him to achieve his goal. But if he is overly ambitious in his assumptions, he will end up investing too little money toward his goal. The penalty for this unfulfilled optimism could be as bad as never meeting his investment goal; or, more likely, he will need to invest painfully high sums as his goal approaches (to make up for the planned for investment returns that never materialized).

Expected Return

Here is where the discussion of market returns in Chapters 1 and 10 come into play. Larry has chosen an investment that tracks the market (has a beta of 1.0), so he can expect roughly market returns. Intermediate government bonds are promising a yield of 14%, so investors must be expecting (demanding!) much more for a risky stock market investment. Based on Table 10-2, when bond rates are 14%, an investment with a beta of 1.0 could be expected to return a compound average quarterly rate of approximately 4.5%.[4]

If we can expect a 4.5% compound quarterly return, then the quarterly investment required is only $1,401 ($467 monthly). It appears that, based on current inflation and expected investment rates, Larry can set enough aside to meet his goal.

Taxes

But what about taxes? We've assumed a 4.5% quarterly return on investment (before taxes), but then went ahead and used the figure as if taxes had already been taken care of. Unfortunately, we will have to make some provision for taxes—this will obviously make it more difficult to achieve the final investment goal of $150,000 spendable dollars. Suppose Larry is in the 28% tax bracket.[5] There are three basic ways that these taxes might be accounted for, depending on how Larry "shelters" his investment, if at all.

If the investment is made with pre-tax dollars—such as an IRA, 401k, Keogh plan, etc.—all taxes are deferred until withdrawal, on every dollar invested or accumulated. For example, in the plan above, we invested $1,401 and earned 4.5% quarterly, resulting in $150,000 in ten years. But after paying 28% taxes on this, we would only have $108,000 to spend, falling well short of our goal. Thus, to clear $150,000 after taxes, we would need to accumulate a fund of $208,333; paying 28% taxes would cost $58,333, leaving us with our goal. This would require a quarterly investment of $1,946. This seems like too much, but recall that Larry could set aside $400-$500 per month, presumably after taxes. He would need to have $555-$694 available monthly *before* taxes (at 28%) to accomplish this; thus the goal is within his sights.

A second approach would be if investments are made after taxes (unlike above), but that all investment earnings are tax-deferred (as above). Let's see how this would affect our plan above, investing $1,401 to achieve $150,000 in ten years. We would only pay taxes on our $94,000 in profits (having already been taxed on the 40 × $1,401 = $56,000 invested), costing us $26,300 in taxes, and leaving us that much short of our goal. To clear $150,000 as desired, we would need to accumulate $1,700 quarterly toward a $181,900 ten-year goal.[6] Taxable profits on the $68,000 invested total would be $113,900; at a 28% tax rate, we would owe $31,900 in taxes, leaving $150,000 to spend. This $1,700 quarterly requirement is quite a bit over our funds available.

The final approach is "pay as you go." As we earn our 4.5% quarterly return, we would pay a 28% tax on it. Thus, our after tax earnings would only be 72% of 4.5%, or 3.24%. At this lower rate, it would be much harder to accumulate $150,000. Quarterly investments of $1,883 would be needed to achieve our goal;[7] this is well above Larry's limited budget.

What will Larry's tax situation be? This problem is unlikely to fit the first scenario, as it is not a retirement goal. If we assume that his investments take place outside of a tax-sheltered account, then it seems like the last scenario applies: pay taxes as you go. Thus, we will use the 3.24% quarterly rate of return for planning purposes (4.5%, less 28% of that for taxes, as above). In reality, though, our stock index fund investment will provide some tax deferral benefit. You only pay taxes on mutual fund distributions, and on gains when you sell. Much of our ongoing return from the fund will be *unrealized* or paper gains, which will be deferred and taxed as in the second scenario above (and at the capital gains rate, as well). Thus, the reality will lie between the last two, "tax-deferred" and "pay-as-you-go" scenarios described above. We'll use the latter approach, reducing our planned rate of return to 3.24% quarterly, as it is the most conservative approach. To achieve the broadest possible coverage, we'll go back and look at the first approach (tax-sheltered retirement fund) later, when we use the value averaging strategy.

IMPLEMENTING DOLLAR COST AVERAGING

After considering taxes, Larry's investment problem seems difficult; recall that $1,883 would be needed each quarter, if a level investment approach (pure-DCA) is used. At this point, we need to specify a particular investment approach. First, we will plan and implement Larry's accumulation plan using dollar cost averaging. After working through ten years of the DCA approach, we will examine the use of value averaging to conclude the chapter.

1981: Setting Up DCA

Armed with the information estimated above, we are prepared to set up a dollar cost averaging plan to achieve our goal. Let's review the important figures at our disposal, December 31, 1981:

$ 57,830	Current cost of land
$150,000	Expected cost of land in 10 years (goal)
$ 1,500	Limit on funds available for quarterly investment
10%	Expected annual inflation rate
4.50%	Expected pre-tax quarterly return on fund investment
3.24%	Expected after-tax quarterly return
40	Number of quarters to accumulate goal

We've already investigated setting up a level-DCA approach, but we found out that it required $1,883/quarter, which was too much current income to set aside. We failed to account for the fact that Larry may be able to increase his investment contributions over time. Thus, we can begin with a lower, more reasonable initial DCA contribution, and then increase it regularly over the ten years to keep up with inflation. This "growth-adjusted" DCA strategy has been discussed often in earlier chapters.

How much would Larry need to start investing if he decided to increase his investment contributions at the inflation rate? For that, we turn to formula #4-15, the "Approximate Growth-Adjusted DCA Formula." The variable we will want to solve for is C, the initial quarter's DCA amount or investment contribution. We have already estimated V_t to be $150,000, and know t to be 40 quarters.

The other input, R, is the average rate; $R = (r + g) \div 2$, is calculated by averaging the quarterly expected rate of investment return, and the quarterly rate at which you plan to increase the DCA amount. Here, if we average the $r = 3.24\%$ after-tax return with the $g = 2.50\%$ planned growth in DCA amount,[8] we get $R = 2.87\%$. This calculates to a growth factor of 124.05; that is, if our initial DCA amount, C, is $1, our expected accumulated total after 40 quarters is $124.05. Since we plan to accumulate $150,000, we must divide that by the growth factor, arriving at an initial quarterly DCA amount of $C = \$1,209.$[9]

This falls in the low end of our available investment range of $400-$500 per month, so Larry could invest more, to be conservative. He could also reduce some of the assumed inputs, to allow less chance of falling short of expectations. For example, Larry could reduce his expected after-tax return on the fund to $r = 3.00\%$, and reduce his required increase in future contributions to $g = 2.00\%$, and still get a reasonable required investment of $C = \$1,397$. Larry feels that we have been quite conservative already in our various assumptions, and decides to stick with $C = \$1,209$.

Larry should begin by investing $1,209 for the initial quarter, and then should increase this amount each quarter by 2.5% (to $1,239, $1,270, $1,302, etc., subsequently). To keep things simpler, Larry would prefer to only adjust his investment amount each year. If he increases his investment by 10% at the end of the year, that leaves all his quarterly contributions lower than they should be. Thus, he decides to start with an amount 5% higher than his initial "requirement" and stay with it; this would be $1,270. At the beginning of the year, he is investing 5% over his goal; but as his goal increases over the course of the year, he is investing 5% under his goal by the end of the year, as he left the investment amount unchanged. At that time, he would increase the investment amount by 10% (to $1,397), leaving it there for the entire second year. So, Larry puts $1,270 into the mutual fund on the last day of 1981, and hopes for the best. He also sends off for some drawings and floor plans for several cabin designs that struck his fancy.

1982-1983 Investment Results

The DCA investment results for the first eight quarters are recorded in Table 11-3. The first entry shows that there was no investment balance in 1981, until the first investment of $1,269.61 at a price of $15.52 per share at the end of December.

The March 1982 entry shows the investment performance over the first quarter. The fund price fell by -8.3% from $15.52 to $14.23; combined with a distribution (income dividends and realized capital gains) of 1.157%, the total return on investment for the period was -7.2%. The distribution of $14.68, taxable at 28%, results in a tax of $4.11, leaving $10.57 available for reinvestment. All of this results in an investment balance of $1,174.66 just prior to the March 31, 1982 investment of $1,269.61.

Continuing like this through the remaining seven quarters, Larry's investment fund grows to $13,359.78 by December 31, 1983. His eight quarterly investments totalled $10,664.72, but his tax basis would be higher due to the $888.74 of total reinvested distributions. The tax basis is $11,553.46, so the "paper gains" yet to be taxed are $1,806.32 (taxes on these gains are deferred until they are realized, when the fund shares are sold).

1983: Reassessment and Readjustment

There were many changes and surprises over the first two years of Larry's investment plan. First of all, his index fund did considerably better than he had expected—after eight quarters, Larry had expected a fund balance of only $12,130.[10] Instead, he has $13,360 of value built up, a nice surprise of $1,230 extra.

Also, inflation has been kind to him; prices only increased by 3.87% and 3.80% in 1982 and 1983, as opposed to the 10% expected inflation rate. Thus, in current dollars, the

TABLE 11-3 DCA Results—First Two Years					
Period	Fund Price	Distrib. Rate	Distrib. Reinvest	Begin Balance	DCA Invest
Dec 81	$15.52	--	--	$ 0.00	$1269.61
Mar 82	$14.23	1.157%	$ 10.57	$1174.66	$1269.61
Jun 82	$13.99	1.259%	$ 22.15	$2425.19	$1269.61
Sep 82	$15.36	1.257%	$ 33.44	$4090.07	$1269.61
Dec 82	$17.56	3.512%	$135.51	$6262.86	$1396.57
Mar 83	$19.08	1.034%	$ 57.04	$8379.47	$1396.57
Jun 83	$20.93	.957%	$ 67.37	$10791.30	$1396.57
Sep 83	$20.70	.851%	$ 74.64	$12128.58	$1396.57
Dec 83	$19.70	5.011%	$488.02	$13359.78	??

plot of land costing $57,830 in 1981 cost $60,070 in 1982, and $62,350 at the end of 1983.

Expected inflation over the next eight years has abated as well. Using last year's inflation, we could expect 3.8% inflation again in 1984. Based on promised T-bill rates for 1984 (less 2%), we could project a 7.85% inflation rate. Using the longer term T-bond yields (less 3%), a 8.41% inflation prediction would result. Weighting the latter prediction most heavily, these indicators average out to an estimated expected inflation rate of 7%. Applying this 7% estimate to the current land price of $62,350 and compounding for eight years, our investment goal for 1991 is only **$107,130.**

Most of the news is good. Our investment goal has been revised downward considerably due to reduced inflation, and we are further along toward our investment goal than expected due to a spate of good market returns. But not all the news is good. In this lower rate environment, expected or required rates of return on both stocks and bonds are lower as well. Based on the

11.41% intermediate government bond rate, the average return that we can expect on our index fund investment can be estimated from Table 10-2 to be about 3.9% quarterly (down from 4.5% before). Thus, while our destination is much closer than we expected, the speed limit on the road to that destination has been substantially reduced.

Given all these major changes and their obvious impact on the original investment plan, the time has come to readjust the plan in order to re-target our goal. This process of regular readjustment was discussed in detail in Chapter 4. Larry planned to readjust his figures every two years, based on new information and unexpected changes in his goals, his investment success, and his expected future returns.

Given these new estimates to work with, we can recalculate the investment amounts required to meet our new goal. We should account for the expected growth in our existing "pot" of money already accumulated, and then calculate the future investments required to get us the rest of the way to the final goal. This procedure is described in Chapter 4.

Our $13,360 worth of funds already accumulated should grow at an expected rate of return of 3.9% quarterly (before taxes). Adjusted for 28% taxes, this leaves a 2.81% quarterly return. Over the 32 quarters remaining, our "1st pot" of money here would grow to about $32,430 by 1991.

This analysis leaves out one seemingly minor point on taxes that must be considered. In the section above, we note that Larry has already accumulated, but not yet paid taxes on, $1,806.32 of "paper gains" that have not yet been realized. The taxes on that amount are about $506 and must be accounted for at some point. I see at least a couple of ways to deduct these tax liabilities from our investment results. At one extreme, it is possible to defer taxation of these gains until sale in 1991. This would result in a 1991 tax bill of $506, reducing our final investment amount of $32,430 to $31,924. At the other extreme, we could "charge ourselves" for the taxes now, since all of our other tax calculations are "pay-as-you-go." Thus, of the $13,360 we currently have, we could treat $506 of it as really belonging to the I.R.S., leaving us with $12,854 now, after taxes. Over the time remaining, this would be expected to grow to about **$31,201**, even lower than above. This is a more conservative approach, and I will use it for all of Larry's calculations. Admittedly, this unrealized tax obligation does not make a huge difference; but if we consistently ignore such tax liabilities, we will consistently find ourselves short of our goals when the tax bill finally arrives.

So after a conservative adjustment for taxes, we expect the current investments to grow to about $31,200, leaving us $75,930 short of our final goal. We now have 32 quarters to build up an investment of that size. We will want to solve DCA Formula #4-15 for C, the initial investment amount that we will increase by g each quarter. With inflation expected to be 7.0%, we will use 1.75% for g, as Larry will increase his investment over time at the expected inflation rate. We have already determined the expected quarterly after-tax rate of return on investment to be $r = 2.81\%$. Averaging the two, we get $R = 2.28\%$. We know that the target value for this "second pot" of future investments is $V = \$75,930$, and that there are $t = 32$ quarters remaining. The calculation, with these numbers, simplifies to: $75,930 = C \times 65.8$, or $C = \textbf{\$1,154}$.

So now, after readjusting for the many surprises and changes in 1983, we find that a quarterly investment of $1,154 is all that is required to meet the investment goal. Note that we had been investing $1,397 per quarter throughout 1983; Larry is prepared to (and expected to) invest over $1,400 per quarter and would prefer to invest more than the $1,154 needed.

There are several approaches to dealing with this very good news. One obvious choice is to simply keep setting aside larger amounts (say, $1,454), applying $1,154 to the DCA plan for the land, and having $300 available to start investing toward a separate goal, perhaps a fishing boat. A second approach, as discussed in Chapter 4, is to trade up to a higher investment amount ($C\!\!\uparrow$) for now, but growing it slower ($g\!\!\downarrow$) in the future.

If we held the investment amount the same as last year ($1,397), the quantity $(1 + R_f)^{32}$ would have to equal 1.70 (see formula #4-16). This would mean that R would have to be 1.67% in the future; we could only get this with $r = 2.81\%$ by averaging it with a projected growth of $g = 0.53\%$. That is, if we invest $1,397 now, we would only have to grow our investment contributions by about .53%/quarter, or 2% per year, instead of the 7% inflation rate as planned above. A third approach, even more conservative, would be to reduce our projected return on investment (r), and recalculate the required investment. A final alternative is to "downshift risk" by transferring some of our "excess funds" over to a safer investment.

This final alternative is the approach that Larry chooses to use during each biannual readjustment process. His logic is that he wants to be fairly sure that he will achieve his investment goal in 1991. This is obviously quite difficult to assure when using a risky equity investment. As 1991 draws near, Larry should be more and more nervous about having his entire stash sitting in a fund with potentially high price swings. If he can afford to, he will occasionally shift some of his investment into low-risk vehicles, such as a money-market fund.[11] By downshifting risk, he trades away some of the expected high returns (of equity) for less risk and less chance of disappointment. In addition, moving money from equity funds to money market funds involves a sale of the equity funds, which results in a tax realization (more on this later).

Larry decides to tailor such an approach to his needs. He is willing to have his quarterly investment increase at the inflation rate, so if C is calculated to be lower than expected (as it was here), he is willing to shift accumulated money over to a money market fund, which would require a higher investment amount (C) to make up for the lower expected return. He decides, however, to never shift more than half of his equity fund over to the money market fund at one time.

How would this work at the 1983 readjustment? Recall that Larry's 1983 quarterly contribution was $1,397; given the

7% expected inflation rate, he would be willing for that amount to go up to $1,495 for 1984. As we saw above, though, good fortune has had the result of lowering the required quarterly contribution to $1,154, if we keep all of the money sitting where it is, in the high-risk, high-return equity fund. Suppose that we move 50% of our available money to the money market fund, which is yielding only 1.64% per quarter after taxes (or, 2.28% pre-tax) right now. Out of our account balance of $13,360, we move $6,680 to a money market fund.

Taxes will complicate this. Recall our $1,806 of accumulated paper gains? If we sell half our investment, we will realize half of these gains, and must pay taxes of 28% of the $903 realized profit—a $253 tax bill. Thus, we will have $6,427 moved to the money market fund after accounting for these taxes.

The "1st pot" of money now consists of a $6,427 money market fund, with an expected quarterly return of 1.64%; and, a $6,680 index fund (conservatively "worth" only $6,427 after accounting for taxes due on unrealized gains, as discussed above), with an expected quarterly return of 2.81%. All of this is after taxes. At these rates, the funds should grow to $10,820 and $15,600, respectively, for a total 1991 value of $26,420. Note that this is considerably lower than the $31,200 expected future value arrived at above, where we kept all money in the equity fund. To achieve our 1991 goal of $107,130, we will need to accumulate about $80,700 over the next 32 quarters. This requires a growing quarterly investment with an initial value of $C = $**1,226**. This is more than $1,154, but still considerably less than Larry can afford.

As we are only increasing the investment amount annually, we will adjust the beginning amount upwards by half the inflation rate, and then wait a year before increasing the amount for inflation. Thus, we will begin with a $1,269 investment each quarter until December 1984, at which time we will increase the amount by 7% to $1,358 per quarter until December 1985. At that time, we will again readjust the investment plan. The above discussion on the 1983 plan readjustment in summarized in the numbers in Table 11-4 below.

The 1985 Readjustment

After our leisurely and detailed stroll through the initial set-up and the 1983 readjustment, we can quickly move through the high points of the next readjustment in 1985. The key points for each readjustment are summarized in logical order in Table 11-4 below.

By the end of 1985, inflation had continued at well below its expected pace, bringing the current price of the land up to $67,260. A rough estimate of future expected inflation is 4.8% at this time, giving an expected goal of only $89,110 in 1991 dollars. The accumulated investment in the index fund has grown to $22,046 (including paper profits of $3,615), while the 1983 investment in the money market fund has grown gradually to $7,309.

These already accumulated investments will grow over the 24 quarters remaining until 1991. The money market fund is currently yielding 1.36% after taxes; it is expected to amount to $10,110 by 1991. As for the equity investment, accounting for potential taxes of $1,012 on the paper profits, there is $21,034 really available in the index fund after taxes. The expected quarterly investment return should be 3.3%, or almost 2.38% after taxes. At this rate, the money in the index fund should grow to $36,970 by 1991. Combined with the money market fund, we can expect roughly $47,080 by 1991 from our current investments (assuming no additional transfer to the money market fund to "downshift risk"). This would leave a shortfall of $42,030 to be accrued with additional investments over the next 24 quarters.

To solve for the required investment amount, we need to determine the expected value for R. By averaging the quarterly inflation rate of 1.2% with the after-tax r of 2.376%, we get a value of $R = 1.788\%$. By solving for C using $t = 24$, we get a required investment of only $C = \$1,145$ per quarter.

This value is quite a bit lower than we expected, due again to our good fortune in terms of low inflation and high investment returns. Larry can again take an opportunity to reduce risk by shifting some investment funds over into the money market fund, while still maintaining enough upside to achieve his goal.

We shift 50% of his index fund money over to the money market fund, adding $10,517 to his balance after paying gains taxes. This transaction results in $17,826 in the money market fund, and leaves $11,023 in the index fund ("worth" $10,517 after a provision for taxing paper profits). At the expected investment rates on the two funds, they should yield respective balances of $24,670 and 18,480, or a total of $43,150, by 1991.

We still need to fund the shortfall of $45,960 with future investments. Using $R = 1.788\%$ and $t = 24$ as above, the required investment is calculated to be $C = \mathbf{\$1,252}$. Using this as the base, Larry invests $1,282 each quarter in 1986, and plans to increase this by inflation to $1,343 for 1987.

And So On and So On . . .

The last couple of readjustments, in December 1987 and 1989, are also shown in detail in Table 11-4. Low inflation continues to temper our investment goal, keeping it down in the $85,000 range in 1991 dollars. The stock market crash of 1987 puts a damper on Larry's investment success, but the plan still performs well enough to allow a transfer of 20% of the index fund into the money market at the end of 1987, while still keeping the required investment amount down to $C = \$1398$, the same as his investment way back in 1983. At this point, he has moved well over half of his investment funds over to the

TABLE 11-4: Summary of DCA Plan Set-up and Readjustment					
Date	Dec 81	Dec 83	Dec 85	Dec 87	Dec 89
Years Remaining	10	8	6	4	2
Qtrs Remaining (t)	**40**	**32**	**24**	**16**	**8**
Current Land Price	57,830	62,350	67,260	71,020	77,610
Expected Inflation Rate ($g \times 4$)	10.0%	7.0%	4.8%	4.8%	5.0%
Expected 1991 Price (Goal)	150,000	107,130	89,110	85,670	84,870
Index Fund grew to		$13,360	$22,046	$23,289	$42,439
MMF grew to			$ 7,309	$19,555	$27,129
Qtrly Exp. Return: MMF (after-tax) Stock, Pre-tax **After-tax (r)**	4.5% **3.24%**	1.64% 3.9% **2.81%**	1.36% 3.3% **2.38%**	1.34% 3.2% **2.30%**	1.55% 3.1% **2.23%**
% transfer to MMF		50%	50%	20%	50%
$ transfer to MMF: Pre-tax After-tax		$ 6,680 $ 6,427	$11,023 $10,517	$ 4,658 $ 4,565	$21,219 $19,710
MMF Total Balance: Now Expected, 1991		$ 6,427 $10,820	$17,826 $24,670	$24,120 $29,830	$46,839 $52,970
Index Fund Balance: Now Now (tax-adjusted) Expected, 1991		$ 6,680 $ 6,427 $15,600	$11,023 $10,517 $18,480	$18,631 $18,262 $26,290	$21,219 $19,710 $23,520
Total "Pot 1": Expected 1991 **Shortfall (V)**	**150,000**	26,420 **80,710**	43,150 **45,960**	56,120 **29,550**	76,490 **9,070**
$R = (r+g) \div 2$	**2.87%**	**2.28%**	**1.79%**	**1.75%**	**1.74%**
C calculated	**$1,209**	**$1,226**	**$1,252**	**$1,398**	**$ 988**
Qtrly Investment: 1st Year 2nd Year	$1,270 $1,397	$1,269 $1,358	$1,282 $1,343	$1,432 $1,501	$1,013 $1,063

money market, and is thus not exposed to much risk of falling short of his investment goal.

The final readjustment in 1989 reflects substantial success in the index fund over 1988 and 1989. By accumulating a total of almost $70,000 already by 1989, Larry can essentially "coast" for the remaining two years. Even when he transfers half of his risky investment over to the money market fund, and accounts for taxes, he is still so close to the final goal that he only requires quarterly investments of $C = \$988$. With two years left, Larry is positioned well with about \$47,000 in the money market fund and about \$20,000 after taxes in the index fund. In reality, it would probably make sense to readjust the plan one more time as we come down to the last year, just to make sure that the final goal stays in sight. But Larry's approach at this point is so conservative, and his financial slack (in terms of being able to increase his investment contribution over the \$988 required) so great, that there is really little room for concern.

Wrapping It Up: 1991 Results

By 1991, the price of the land which was Larry's brass ring had risen to **\$84,870**; no real surprises in the last four years or so. His money market fund investment rose in value to \$51,970, and his index fund investment rose to \$36,250, giving a total investment fund of \$88,220. But since much of the index fund value represented paper profits (capital gains) of \$8,446, there were taxes due in the amount of \$3,102 on these gains. This reduces the investment fund to a spendable, after-tax amount of **\$85,120**, just more than enough to cover the cost of his goal.[12] Larry's gone fishin'.

This concludes the detailed example of the actual planning and implementation of a DCA strategy. I hope this has provided you with a thorough exposition of the problems, judgements, pitfalls, and techniques required to achieve your own investment goal. Larry's experience brings to light the importance of planning, making reasoned estimates, being flexible, dealing up front with taxes, and readjusting the plan on a regular basis.

Now we will turn to the same investment problem, using the alternate strategy of value averaging.

IMPLEMENTING VALUE AVERAGING

We'll now follow Larry's journey through this same investment scenario to observe the issues and techniques involved in planning and implementing with value averaging. Much of the discussion above, on setting up a DCA plan, will also apply here. The basic 1981 information is the same: the land price of $57,800 is still expected to cost $150,000 in 1991 at a 10% expected inflation rate; the pre-tax and after-tax quarterly expected returns on the index fund are 4.5% and 3.24%, respectively; Larry still has a rough idea that his available after-tax investment funds are in the $1,200-$1,500 range (quarterly) now, although he would expect that contribution to grow with inflation over time. The main difference is that here, Larry chooses to use value averaging in formulating his investment plan. One other difference here is that we will use Larry's tax-sheltered retirement account—such as his 401k plan, which uses pre-tax investment money and postpones all taxes until withdrawal.

Establishing the Value Path

The simple formula that takes account of expected market returns and the (on average) increasing investment contributions is the *value path*. As described in Chapter 5, its role is to set up a target value for every point in time between now and your final goal, resulting in reaching that goal in the time available. The VA Formula, #5-19, is reproduced in the box at the end of this chapter.

We've already discussed all the inputs above; there are some changes here, in consideration of the different tax status. There are $t = 40$ quarters. Since the 401k investment is made with pre-tax dollars, all taxes are deferred until withdrawal, on every dollar invested or accumulated. Our goal is $150,000; but since we must pay taxes on our entire withdrawal at a 28% rate, we really need to accrue $208,333, to clear $150,000 after paying $58,333 in taxes—thus, $V_{40} = 208,333$ is our investment goal. Also, due to the use of pre-tax dollars, Larry's ability to save $1200-$1500 quarterly *after* taxes translates into about $1550-2100 of *pre-tax* money made available for investment contributions.

Our quarterly expected return on investment, pre-tax, is $r = 4.5\%$. We'll call C the initial contribution; while we cannot determine (as in DCA) future contributions in VA, C is the amount that we will expect to put in, on average, to meet our value goal, after accounting for an investment return on existing shares. To allow this expected investment contribution to increase with inflation over time, we set $g = 2.5\%$, our estimate of the quarterly inflation rate. R, which is simply the average of r and g, is 3.5% here.

Solving the formula to meet our 1991 goal, we get an initial contribution figure of $C =$ **$1,315.48**. This gives a value path formula of:
$$V_t = 1,315.48 \times t \times (1.035)^t$$

This value path solves for the target value we should achieve at every point in time. Starting with $t = 1$, we must invest to achieve a target value of $1,362. Next quarter, we will invest whatever is required to bring our fund value up to $2,818. At $t=40$, we would invest enough to reach our final pre-tax target goal of $208,333.

The timing of this plan is actually a bit conservative, as we are beginning our investment right away ($t = 1$ now, instead of $t = 0$). This means that $t = 40$, our final investment, occurs at September 1991, a quarter before our need. This is good, though, since in neither plan (VA nor DCA) did we want to *need* an investment in December 1991. By making our last investment in the quarter before our goal, we can "coast in" at money market rates with no risk of missing our goal. A much less conservative approach would be to recompute C, letting $t = 41$; this would require an unknown and potentially huge cash investment in December 1991, which is probably not what Larry wants.

The plan implementation begins with a $1,362 investment on the last day of 1981. The first eight quarters of the VA plan is shown in Table 11-5. Any dividends or fund distributions are reinvested; the "Beginning Balance" for March 82 reflects the actual value (which was set to equal the value target) in December 81, less the decrease in price, plus fund distributions. Due to losses in the fund, the March and June investments are slightly larger than expected; the opposite is true over the next year, as the fund is providing above-expected gains that contribute toward the value target (making our investment lower than "planned"). After two years we "rest" and reevaluate our inputs, assumptions, and check to see if our plan needs to be readjusted.

1983: Readjusting the VA Plan

As in the previous (DCA) example, much can change over a few years. The two major changes that will affect the value averaging trajectory toward the goal are changes in the goal itself and changes in the expected rate of return. Inflation and interest rates dropped considerably over the 1982-3 period, creating a new investment landscape for us to traverse.

Based on our discussion of inflation from the DCA section, our new expected 1991 after-tax goal is $107,132. Allowing for 28% taxes, our pre-tax goal is now $V = $148,800$, down about $60,000 from before. We should now be "further along" our value path than we had expected.

But the expected return on our investments, as well as our inflation or growth adjustment, have dropped as well. The new quarterly figures of $r = 3.9\%$ and $g = 1.75\%$ give an average rate of $R = 2.825\%$.

Due to the new goal and the new expected return, we are effectively on a new value path (which we have yet to cal-

TABLE 11-5 VA Results—First Two Years				
Period	Fund Price	Value Target	Beginning Balance	VA Investment
Dec 81	$15.52	$1,362	0	$1,362
Mar 82	$14.23	$2,818	$1,264	$1,554
Jun 82	$13.99	$4,375	$2,806	$1,569
Sep 82	$15.36	$6,038	$4,859	$1,179
Dec 82	$17.56	$7,812	$7,115	$697
Mar 83	$19.08	$9,702	$8,569	$1,133
Jun 83	$20.93	$11,716	$10,736	$980
Sep 83	$20.70	$13,858	$11,687	$2,171

culate). It's a value path that, at $R = 2.825\%$, will grow to $V = \$107,132$ over the next 32 quarters. Treating December 1983 as our 1st quarter, we can go back and use our September 1983 value of $13,858 as our "0th quarter," or starting point. Now we simply have to adjust for the fact that, on this new value path, we have a $13,858 "head-start."

That's where the VA Readjustment Formula (#5-21) is useful. If we set $T = 32$ as our goal, with $t = 1$ now and $t = 0$ as our starting point, the standard value path formula would give our starting value as $0; we had $13,858 to "start with" last quarter. The readjustment formula simply comes up with a new "time index" for our goal and our starting point (but still keeps them 32 quarters apart). Solving for T with the inputs just discussed, the formula yields $T = 41.4$ as our new time index for our goal. Our starting point is 32 quarters earlier, so last quarter is indexed $t = 9.4$, and right now it is nominally $t = 10.4$. This has little intrinsic meaning, other than that we are effectively already 9.4 periods along the way of a 41.4-period value path, with 32 to go. This is "better" than being only 8 periods into a 40-period value path; more *progress*, so to speak.

The new time index is used to recalculate our figure for C, so that we can calculate our new value path, giving us new targets for each quarter that will achieve our new goal. We know that at our 1991 goal, $T = 41.4$ and $V_T = 148,800$. Using $R = 2.825\%$ and these inputs in the value path formula #5-19, we get $C = \$1,134$. This is the C we will use to create the value path formula. But what does it mean? Recall the C simply designates the average expected investment contribution at $t = 0$; this contribution grows each quarter by rate g. Thus, by quarter 10.4 (December 1983, which is now), this expected contribution is now $(1 + g)^{10.4}$ times as large, or, $\$1,358$—and still growing. Note that this figure is roughly as large as our initial quarterly value from back in 1981. The fact that the readjusted figure has not increased for inflation is a positive sign of Larry's better-than-expected progress toward his goal.

We use the $C = \$1,134$ figure, the new time index, and the value path formula, to compute a new value path that gets us to our goal in time. We can first put in $t = 9.4$ to check that the required value for last quarter was $\$13,858$, which was in fact the value.[13] Our current target for December 1983 ($t = 10.4$) is $\$15,765$, increasing up to $\$32,050$ in September 1985, and on to $\$148,800$ in eight years when we reach our goal.

Future VA Readjustments

We will readjust again in December 1985; and 1987; and 1989. The mechanics and the impact of these readjustments are shown in Table 11-6. The increasing values of T and decreasing values of C indicate that reduced inflation is moving Larry along toward his goal a bit quicker than expected.

TABLE 11-6 Summary of VA Plan Set-up and Readjustment					
Date	Dec 81	Dec 83	Dec 85	Dec 87	Dec 89
Qtrs Remaining	40	32	24	16	8
Time-Index:					
"Start," prior Qtr	0	9.4	19.0	29.5	37.3
Current Qtr	1	10.4	20.0	30.5	38.3
Goal Qtr, $T=$	40	41.4	43.0	45.5	45.3
Quarterly Figures:					
g Expected Inflation	2.50%	1.75%	1.2%	1.2%	1.25%
r Expected Return	4.5%	3.90%	3.3%	3.2%	3.1%
R	3.50%	2.825%	2.25%	2.2%	2.175%
"Starting Value," Prior Quarter, V_t	$ 0	$13,858	$32,050	$54,426	$82,374
Expected 1991 Price:					
Pre-tax, V_T	$208,333	$148,800	$123,760	$118,980	$118,830
After-tax	$150,000	$107,130	$89,110	$85,670	$84,870
C calculated	$1,315	$1,134	$1,106	$974	$990
Expected Qtrly Contributions over next 2 years: $C \times (1+g)^t$	$1,350 -$1,600	$1,360 -$1,530	$1,400 -$1,530	$1,400 -$1,520	$1,590 -$1,740
Value Path, 8 Qtrs:					
D	$ 1,362	$15,765	$34,497	$57,512	$86,422
M	$ 2,818	$17,768	$37,037	$60,708	$90,607
J	$ 4,375	$19,872	$39,675	$64,017	$94,934
S	$ 6,038	$22,081	$42,412	$67,441	$99,406
D	$ 7,812	$24,399	$45,253	$70,986	$104,027
M	$ 9,702	$26,829	$48,200	$74,653	$108,803
J	$11,716	$29,378	$51,256	$78,448	$113,736
S	$13,858	$32,050	$54,426	$82,374	$118,834

VA Investments

Having set up and occasionally readjusted the value paths, we have yet to look at the actual investment cash flows and performance. The value averaging approach ensures that you will reach your goal, but doesn't tell you anything about what you will need (to invest) to get there. We'll look at two versions of implementing the VA plan: a base case with highly variable investment flows and no controls, and a "smoother" version that simply controls the out-of-pocket investment contributions.

The fund's total return performance and the value path are detailed on the left-hand side of Table 11-7. The center section shows the base case, where you apply value averaging with no controls on your out-of-pocket investment—you invest whatever necessary to achieve your value target. Recall that the average expected quarterly investment at a given point in time is C, adjusted upward for inflation; we'll call this C_t below, where $C_t = C \times (1 + g)^t$. We expect to invest that much each quarter; the money market fund (MMF) will be used to help out where necessary.

Here's the procedure Larry used for moving money around to meet his value target. If there is no money in the MMF, Larry comes up with the entire investment from cash (see Dec81-Sep85). If there are excess funds (as in Dec85-Mar86) they are moved to the MMF. If the funds required are less than expected ($<C_t$), they will be newly invested out of cash (e.g., Jun86, Dec86). Any funds needed over C_t will be taken from the MMF (e.g., Sep86). Finally, if the need is so great that it exhausts the MMF, then any additional requirement to meet the value target will come from cash (as in Dec87 and Sep90).

The final result of the base case was that we ended up with too much money. Even after paying taxes, we still have $16,000 of extra money over and above our $85,600 goal. Some of this is due to a sizable unexpected pot of money in the MMF (discussed below). Another reason is that we set up our value path to reach its goal in Sep91, and then let the funds stay invested, letting the account wander up and down in value (mostly up!) with the market for the rest of the year. It would have made more sense to reduce our risk by shifting our money out of the risky investment (and into the MMF) once we had come close to achieving our goal. It makes even more sense to have done this gradually, "downshifting risk" over at least the last two years of the plan. This philosophy was described and implemented in detail in the DCA section of this chapter.

TABLE 11-7 VA Investment Cash Flows

Quarter	Total Return	Value Target	Value Owned	Base Case—Invest as Necessary			Invest. Limited	
				Difference	Cash Investment	+To -From MMF	Cash Investment	+To -From MMF
Dec 81		$1362	$0	-$1362	$1,362	$0	$1,362	$0
Mar 82	-7.16%	$2818	$1264	-$1554	$1,554	$0	$1,554	$0
Jun 82	-0.43%	$4375	$2806	-$1569	$1,569	$0	$1,569	$0
Sep 82	11.05%	$6038	$4859	-$1179	$1,179	$0	$1,179	$0
Dec 82	17.83%	$7812	$7115	-$697	$697	$0	$697	$0
Mar 83	9.69%	$9702	$8569	-$1133	$1,133	$0	$1,133	$0
Jun 83	10.65%	$11716	$10736	-$980	$980	$0	$980	$0
Sep 83	-0.25%	$13858	$11687	-$2171	$2,171	$0	$2,171	$0
Dec 83	0.18%	$15765	$13883	-$1882	$1,882	$0	$1,882	$0
Mar 84	-2.24%	$17768	$15412	-$2356	$2,356	$0	$2,356	$0
Jun 84	-2.62%	$19872	$17303	-$2569	$2,569	$0	$2,569	$0
Sep 84	9.57%	$22081	$21773	-$308	$308	$0	$308	$0
Dec 84	1.83%	$24399	$22484	-$1915	$1,915	$0	$1,915	$0
Mar 85	9.07%	$26829	$26612	-$217	$217	$0	$217	$0
Jun 85	7.25%	$29378	$28774	-$604	$604	$0	$604	$0
Sep 85	-4.01%	$32050	$28201	-$3849	$3,849	$0	$3,067[1]	$0
Dec 85	16.86%	$34497	$37455	$2958	$0	$2958	$0	$2045
Mar 86	13.96%	$37037	$39313	$2276	$0	$2276	$0	$2276
Jun 86	5.77%	$39675	$39174	-$501	$501	$0	$501	$0
Sep 86	-7.13%	$42412	$36845	-$5567	$1,455	$-4112	$1,455	$-4112
Dec 86	5.47%	$45253	$44732	-$521	$521	$0	$521	$0

TABLE 11-7 VA Investment Cash Flows (cont.)

Quarter	Total Return	Value Target	Value Owned	Difference	Base Case—Invest as Necessary		Invest. Limited	
					Cash Investment	+To -From MMF	Cash Investment	+To -From MMF
Mar 87	21.17%	$48200	$54832	$6632	$0	$6632	$0	$6632
Jun 87	5.02%	$51256	$50620	-$636	$636	$0	$636	$0
Sep 87	6.45%	$54426	$54565	$139	$0	$139	$0	$139
Dec 87	-22.71%	$57512	$42067	-$15445	$7,028	-$8417*	$2,800†	-$7398*
Mar 88	5.64%	$60708	$60758	$50	$0	$50	$2,834†	-$137*
Jun 88	6.47%	$64017	$64636	$619	$0	$619	$2,063†	-$2*
Sep 88	0.34%	$67441	$64233	-$3208	$2,377	-$831*	$2,902†	$0*
Dec 88	2.98%	$70986	$69450	-$1536	$1,520	-$16*	$1,850	$0*
Mar 89	7.04%	$74653	$75982	$1328	$0	$1328	$0	$1328
Jun 89	8.79%	$78448	$81214	$2766	$0	$2766	$0	$2766
Sep 89	10.58%	$82374	$86751	$4377	$0	$4377	$0	$4377
Dec 89	2.02%	$86422	$84035	-$2387	$1,593	-$794	$1,593	-$794
Mar 90	-3.07%	$90607	$83772	-$6835	$1,613	-$5222	$1,613	-$5222
Jun 90	6.21%	$94934	$96236	$1302	$0	$1302	$0	$1302
Sep 90	-13.76%	$99406	$81872	-$17534	$13,247	-$4287*	$3,307†	-$4287*
Dec 90	8.88%	$104027	$108234	$4207	$0	$4207	$3,348†	-$86*
Mar 91	14.47%	$108803	$119078	$10276	$0	$10276	$0	$6633
Jun 91	-0.29%	$113736	$108492	-$5245	$1,716	-$3529	$1,716	-$3529
Sep 91	5.28%	$118834	$119744	$910	$0	$910	$0	$910
Dec 91	8.34%			Final Value	$128,748	$12,572	$128,748	$4,216
				Total, After Taxes	$101,750		$95,734	
				IRR (annual), After-tax	11.58%		11.82%	

* MMF exhausted, except for token interest.   † Fund value temporarily below target value.

Note one serious problem with this "uncontrolled" approach—the cash investment requirements are too variable and sometimes unreasonably high. Ignoring the flows that are simply moving back and forth between the index fund and the MMF, we focus on the column headed *Cash Investment*. On three occasions (Sep85, Dec87, and Sep90), the cash investment required seems too high, due to steep market downturns. As the market rebounds, much of this invested cash ends up parked in the MMF. This is one reason why the base case "overshoots" the value target, as over $12,000 of "extra money" is parked in the MMF by our Dec91 goal.

Larry decided to take a more controlled approach to investing cash into the plan, as he desired more investment stability; this approach is detailed in the last two columns of Table 11-7. He decided to limit his out-of-pocket investment to $2 \times C_t$ (double the expected amount).[14] The first example of this is in Sep85, where the value target called for $3,849 to be invested, and there was as yet no MMF built up. Adjusted for inflation, the expected investment that quarter was about $1,534—double that was $3,067, the limit of Larry's investment. Notice (in the second-last column of Table 11-7) that this is what he invested, leaving him temporarily short of his value target. This shortage is made up during the next investment period. By looking at the "problem areas" of Dec87 and Sep90, you can see how this restriction smooths out the sizable investment requirements after exhausting the MMF. Not only does this spread the investment requirement over a few periods, but it also gives later market recoveries a chance to "kick in some of the needed dollars," as in Dec90-Mar91.

The results of this plan are not only smoother and lower cash investments, but also less excess money parked in the MMF as we reach our final goal. Here, Larry ends up with only one-third as much extra MMF money in Dec91; he only overshoots his goal by about $10,000, most of which is due to an unexpectedly high market return in the quarter after we had achieved our goal (this risk can be removed, as discussed above). The annualized return on investment was 11.82% after taxes with this version of the strategy, slightly higher than the uncontrolled version with its more volatile cash flows.

There are obviously many other possible approaches Larry could have taken to planning, readjusting, controlling, and implementing his VA strategy. We've only looked at two methods of controlling cash flows; create methods of readjusting and controlling the plan that you can be comfortable with.

SUMMARY

With these detailed DCA and VA examples, I hope I've given you plenty of real-world issues to think about, and maybe even answered a few of your questions about implementation. There are as many ways to achieve your investment goals as there are investors. With whatever method you choose, I hope you have as much success as Larry did.

What broad lessons can we learn from Larry's experience? Being flexible is good, but being flexible with a plan is better. Taxes may not be fun to think about them, but you'll either work them into your plan or else have an incredibly nasty surprise lurking between you and your goal. Ditto with inflation. Don't be scared to make educated guesses (we've called them "estimates" and "expectations"), but be prepared to reevaluate them on a regular basis.

KEY FORMULAS

Lump-Sum Investment

$$V_t = C \times (1+r)^t \qquad (4\text{--}3)$$

Periodic Investments

$$V_t = C_{end} \times \frac{1}{r} \left[(1+r)^t - 1\right] \qquad (4\text{--}4)$$

Approximate Growth-Adjusted DCA Formula

$$V_t \approx C \times t \times (1+R)^t \qquad (4\text{--}15)$$

$$\text{where } R_f = \frac{r+g}{2}$$

DCA Readjustment Formula

$$\frac{V_T - V_t \times (1+r)^{T-t}}{C_t \times (T-t)} \approx (1+R_f)^{T-t} \qquad (4\text{--}16)$$

$$\text{where } R_f = \frac{r + g_f}{2}$$

VA Value Path Formula

$$V_t = C \times t \times (1+R)^t \quad \text{where } R = \frac{r+g}{2} \qquad (5\text{--}19)$$

VA Readjustment Formula

$$T = \frac{n}{1 - \dfrac{V_t}{V_T} \times (1+R)^n} \qquad (5\text{--}21)$$

ENDNOTES

1.   The annuity formula assumes end-of-period investments. If we account for the investment being made at the beginning of the month, we get an extra 1%, or one month's compounding (see formula #4-5); the result is then about $93,000.
2.   Accounting for beginning-of-month investment, the result would be over $116,000.
3.   Or about $1930/quarter, based on beginning-of-quarter investment timing. For simplicity of calculations, we will compute required investment amounts based on end-of-period investments. This will result in a conservative approach, because required investments will be calculated to be slightly higher than necessary.
4.   The 14% bond rate is off the chart; the quarterly figure calculated as 4.5% could be approximated by extrapolating the numbers in Table 10-2. I know this (roughly 20% annually) expected return seems huge by today's standards; but remember how likely today's 3% money market rates seemed back in 1981!
5.   Actually, tax "brackets" changed several times over this 10-year period. The "readjustment" process followed later in the chapter deals with changing tax rates quite well; but, for simplicity, we will keep Larry in the 28% bracket throughout the decade.
6.   How did we get this figure of $181,900? Trial-and-error will get you there, but so will a little algebra. Let G be our unknown pre-tax investment goal. Our "profits" will be the difference between G and our investment, which will be $$C$ for n periods; taxes at 28% of profits will amount to: Tax = $.28 \times (G-nC)$. We also want to have $150,000 after reducing G by taxes, so:

$$150000 = G - .28 \times (G-nC); \text{ rearranging,}$$
$$150000 = .72G + .28nC$$

If we knew C, the required periodic investment, we would be done; but, C depends on our unknown goal, G. Recall that C is related to G by the annuity factor, $A=[(1+r)^r-1]/r$ (see formula 4-40): $C = G/A$
       Substituting for C, $150000 = .72G + .28nG/A$
       Grouping G's, $150000 \div (.72+.28n/A) = G$
Here, since $r=4.5\%$, the annuity factor is A=107.03, and $n=40$. Substituting, $G = 150000/.82464 = $ **$181,897**

7. Note the difference in these last two methods of $183 (= $1883 - $1700). This is the value of the tax deferral, as opposed to having to pay taxes on income as you earn it.

8. This is based on the 10% annual inflation rate. The 2.50% quarterly rate ignores compounding to keep things simple. Minor approximations like these are inconsequential, given the number of other approximations and estimations required by this, or any other investment planning process.

9. Using the "exact" DCA formula #4-9 gives a slightly higher result of $C=\$1,240$.

10. Simply set $t=8$ in the DCA Formula #4-15, yielding $V_8=\$12,130$.

11. Of course, he could choose to invest in a truly "fixed-income" investment, such as an 8-year zero-coupon bond that would mature in 1991. This would avoid any "investment risk," but would leave him totally exposed to "inflation risk." Recall that unexpected bad news about investment returns is only one reason why he could fail to meet his final goal. The other (just as important) reason is a potential unexpected increase in inflation. An investment locking in a fixed-dollar amount would do nothing to address inflation risk. Since money-market funds, or other short-term investments, carry "floating" interest rates that tend to move with inflation, they may actually be better suited for situations where you're "trying to hit a moving target."

12. The total cash invested into the plan was $51,712 over the 10 years. The internal rate of return, after all taxes, was 2.25% per quarter. That is, on his cash invested in the two funds, Larry earned an average annualized rate of return of 9.32% after taxes.

13. Don't fret if you get a number a few dollars off. None of my calculations were rounded off, even though I'm reporting rounded figures for inputs and outputs in the text.

14. There is actually some logic behind this (2 times the expected amount) restriction. Supposedly, C_t is the cash investment you would expect in a typical quarter. But some quarters you will invest less, perhaps even as low as 0. Other quarters you will invest more—as much as you limit yourself to. By limiting that multiple (of C_t) to 2, you are, in a loose sense, keeping your expected amount in the middle, varying your actual investments around it in a somewhat symmetric way.

A
Final Word 12

The market is a risky place, especially for investors who follow the psychology of the market, jumping in and out at all the wrong times. The introductory material on market risk and return was geared to help you get a feel for the scope of this risk, and how risk and return relate to your investment plan. There appears to be a role for formula strategies to help guide investors through this rocky investment terrain.

We've concentrated on exploring two popular formula strategies: dollar cost averaging and value averaging. Both have a natural mathematical tendency to buy more shares when prices are low and to buy fewer (or sell) shares when prices are high. This reduces the average cost per share below the average share price and enhances rates of return. The inherent return advantage of value averaging does not make it a better investment strategy for everyone. It is a bit more complex and has implicit costs for some investors. We've seen how flexible the strategies can be, and how you might use them to achieve a target investment goal over a specific period of time.

A few final points need to be made about "mechanical" investment strategies, such as dollar cost averaging and value averaging. Neither one will turn a sow's ear into a silk purse; accumulating a bad investment, no matter the strategy, will result in bad investment returns. Neither of these methods, nor any other formula strategies, nor other "rules" programs will turn stock market investing into a "positive net present value" game, except perhaps as mentioned in the last sections of Chapter 9. Nonetheless, millions of investors subscribe to dollar cost averaging because of its cost reduction and return enhancement characteristics. Now you have shared in analyzing a reasonable alternative to the DCA strategy that may work for you. You certainly won't get rich quick. But it's about as close to "buy low, sell high" as we're going to get without a crystal ball.

Index

American Association of Individual
Investors, 25
Annuities, 60-63
Approximate growth-adjusted DCA
formula, 74
Arithmetic mean, 22-23
Asset allocation strategies, 2

Beta, 23, 174, 180, 181, 190
Black Monday, 151
Bonds, 14, 15, 70
Buy-and-hold strategy, 20, 37

Capital gains tax
cap, 114
deferring, 101-7, 178
Closed-end mutual funds, 188
Compounding, 7, 22-23, 58, 80
Constant-ratio plans, 2
Constant share purchase strategy,
28, 30-36, 37-38, 48, 52, 127,
162-64
Contrarian strategies, 144, 147
Corporate bonds, 14, 15
Correlation coefficient, 190

Deferred gains, 101-2
example of, 102-3, 106-7
Distribution
of eight-year stock returns, 13
of four-year stock returns, 12
of market returns, 9-13
of one-year stock returns, 11, 18
of random stock returns, 124,
125
standard normal, 17

Diversification, 9, 34, 169-70, 174,
175, 190
time, 8, 32, 37-38
Dodge & Cox Stock Fund, 175
Dollar cost averaging (DCA),
25-26, 36-37
definition of, 1-2, 25
example of, 26-28, 49, 202-214
fixed amount, 35-36, 63
growth-adjusted, 71-80
growth equalization of, 35-36
internal rate of return, 28, 29
investment
frequencies, 163, 164, 166-67,
179-80
return and taxes, 200-202
targets, 57-63, 88, 199-200
long-term problems with, 34-36,
71
over five-year periods, 32-34, 49
over one-year periods, 30-32
readjustment of, 63-71, 205-213
spreadsheet for, 83-85
short-term performance of, 28
table, 27, 31, 33, 142
Donnelly, Barbara, 150
Down-shifting risk, 69-71

Effective annual rate, 7, 80
Effective tax rate, 102, 105, 107,
114
Efficient market view, 149, 164, 166
Equity mutual funds, 169-70, 173
Exact growth-adjusted DCA
formula, 72

Expected compound return, 180, 190
Expected return, 15, 18, 119, 126, 180
  and risk, 13-19
  distribution of, 17-19

Fama, Eugene, 149
Financial calculator
  for annuity, 62
  for lump sum, 61
  for readjustment, 67
  for ten-year readjustment, 68
Financial planner notes, 186-89
Fixed-amount rules, 34-35, 47-48
Fixed-dollar strategies, 47-51
Formula strategy, 1-2
  and automatic timing, 21-22
  definition of, 1
  and market timing, 19-22, 161-64
  and overreaction, 160-61
French, Kenneth R., 149
Frontiers of Finance, 159

Geometric mean, 22-23, 190
Government bonds, 14, 15
Growth
  adjustments, 139-42
  equalization, 35-36, 52-53, 166
  strategies, 51-53
Growth-adjusted strategies
  comparison of, 142
  dollar cost averaging, 71-79
  value averaging, 51-53, 88
Guidelines, 185-86

Head-Start VA formula, 91
Herd mentality, avoiding, 2
Histogram
  definition of, 10
  distribution of eight-year stock
    returns, 13

distribution of four-year stock
  returns, 12
distribution of one-year stock
  returns, 11

Index funds, 46, 171-72
Inflation, 14, 15, 38, 71, 184, 197
Inflation adjustments to strategies, 51-52, 197-99
Internal rate of return, 28-29
Investment frequency, 162-64, 185
IRA, 178

Linear strategies (VA), 47-51
Log-normal distribution, 127
Lotus 1-2-3, 83-85, 98-99, 131
Lump-sum investments, 57-59
  example, 59-60, 61

Markese, John, 25
Market
  correction, 19, 151, 160
  efficiency, 164, 166
  level, 1954 figures, 30
  level, 1932 figures, 45
  parameters, 118-19, 134, 179-81
  returns
    distribution of, 9-13
    expected, 15, 119
    over time, 3-6, 8
  risk, 3
    and expected returns, 13-15, 17-19, 121, 180
    and standard deviation, 16, 120, 148
  timing, 9
    and formula strategies, 20-23, 161-64
MATCH, 153-59, 161, 166
Mean, 22-23, 118-19
Mean reversion, 150, 151, 156, 157, 159, 160, 162, 166

Monte Carlo simulations, 126, 129
Mutual funds
  closed-end funds, 188
  expense ratios, 172, 173
  financial planners' notes for,
    186-90
  index, 46, 171-72
  information on specific, 172-75
  retirement account, 177-8, 188
  side, 176-77, 187-88
  using split investment fund, 188-89
  value path for, 178-79, 181
    example, 181-84
  versus stocks, 169-71
Myers, Stuart C., 150, 159

Net average cost, 41, 54
Normal diffusion, 121
Normal distribution, 16, 17, 121,
  127, 130, 133
No-sell value averaging, 107-11,
  142-43, 185

Overreaction, 149-63
  data review of, 151-59
  and mean reversion, 150-51, 159
  why matters, 160-64

Periodic investments. *See* Annuities
  and DCA.
Pure value averaging, 79, 135-38

Quattro Pro, 131

Randomness, 120-21, 147, 152, 166
Random number, 131-33
Random simulation, 123, 126,
  134-47
Random walk, 149-50, 152, 153,
  159, 160-61, 165
Rate of return. *See* Return, rate of.

Readjustment
  of dollar cost averaging, 63-71,
    75-79, 83-85
  of value averaging, 94-95, 97-99,
    184
  of value path, 91, 92
Retirement account, 59, 177-78, 188
Return
  average investment (1926-89), 14
  and compounding, 7, 22-23, 58,
    80, 180
  distribution of, 9-13, 17-19
    random stock, 124, 125
  expected, 15, 18, 119, 126, 180
  over time, 3-6, 8
  rate of
    after tax, 104-5, 180
    annualizing, 7, 58-59
    comparison of, 31, 33, 44, 47,
      52-53, 136, 137, 138, 139, 141,
      142, 143, 145, 146, 163, 164
    for five-year periods, 33
    for one-year periods, 31, 44
    internal (IRR), 29
    no-sell value averaging, 109
    strategy comparisons for, 141
    using various investment
      frequencies, 163, 164
Risk, 3, 189
  and beta, 23, 174-75, 190
  definition of, 23
  down-shifting, 69-71
  and expected returns, 13-15,
    17-19, 180
  premium, 190
  and standard deviation, 17
Riskless investments, 70

Side fund, 176-77, 187-88

Simulations
  constructing, 121-22, 129-33
  example, 122-26
  five-year, results of, 135-44
  twenty-year, results of, 145
  what and how, 118-21
  why, 117-18
Single growth factor DCA formula, 73
Split investment fund, 188-89
Spread, 118
Spreadsheet
  dollar cost averaging
    readjustment, 83-85
  simulation, 129-33
  value averaging readjustment, 97-99
Standard deviation, 16, 17-18, 120, 147
Standard normal random number, 130, 131
Stochastic calculus, 126
Stock index funds, 46, 172
Stock market (also see below)
  consecutive period performance of, 153, 154, 155, 156, 157, 158
  ups and downs of, 10
Stock price levels, 1926-89, monthly, 4
Stock returns
  distribution
    expected future, 18-19
    of eight-year, 13
    of four-year, 12
    of one-year, 11
  historical
    annual, 6
    four-year periods, 8
    monthly, 5
Strategy comparisons, 31-33, 44-47, 52-53, 135-46, 163-64, 193-228

Studentized Range, 133
Summers, Lawrence, 150
SWITCH, 153, 159, 165

Tax considerations
  deferral, 80, 101-3, 114, 178
  limiting, 111-12
  with value averaging, 101-3, 106-8, 110-11, 178
Telephone switch privileges, 170, 172, 178
Time diversification, 8, 32, 37-38
Time value of money, 28-29
Timing, 161-64
  automatic, 21-23
  market, 20-23
Transaction costs, 111-13
Treasury bills, 14-15, 38
Treasury bonds, 14-15, 181, 182
Twentieth Century Select Fund, 173, 181

Uniformly distributed random numbers, 133

Value averaging, 39, 41-43, 53-54, 113
  definition of, 2, 39
  example of, 40, 50, 215-225
  investment frequencies and, 113, 163, 164, 179-80, 185
  long-term performance of, 47-53, 87
  no sell, 107-8, 110-11, 185
  readjustment, 94-95, 184, 217-219
  readjustment spreadsheet for, 97-99
  short-term performance of, 43, 45-46
  tax considerations of, 101-3, 106-8, 110-11
  value path for, 87-95, 215-17

Value path, 51, 52-53, 87, 178-80,
    182-84
  alternate method, 93-94
  example, 181-84
  formula, 88-89
  flexible variations on, 89-92
  readjusting, 91-95, 217-219
  setting up, 87-89, 215-217
Vanguard Index Trust, 175, 193

Vanguard Quantitative Portfolio,
    175
Vanguard Star Fund, 173, 189
Variability, 9, 118, 120, 126
Variable-ratio plans, 2
Volatility, 143-45, 148, 185-86
  (also see *Risk* and *Variability*)

Wall Street Journal, 150

Make Well-Informed No-Load Mutual-Fund Investment Decisions

Kiplinger's Personal Finance Magazine gave *The Individual Investor's Guide to No-Load Mutual Funds* their only 4-Star Rating. Here's what they said:

"If you invest in mutual funds and like to do your own research, chances are you've flipped through a fund guide or two along the way . . . From the American Association of Individual Investors comes this fact-studded book. . . . Individual fund summaries are a data-hound's delight."

Provides up-to-date information on over 600 no-load and very low-load mutual funds, including 5 years of returns, net asset values, distributions, and per share data; 3-year and 5-year average annual returns; performance in bull and bear markets; fund returns and rankings by investment objective; total risk and investment objective risk rankings.

This *Guide to No-Load Mutual Funds* provides the information you need to make well-informed decisions on your mutual fund investments in an easy-to-understand format.   **$24.95 each.**

Order at your local bookstore, use the coupon below, or call 1-800-488-4149.

Name _____   Address _____

City / State / Zip _____   Phone # _____

Check Enclosed Amt _____   Visa / MC # _____

Signature _____   Ship via _____
(Shipped book rate unless othewise indicated)

Quantity   Price   Title   Total

_____ _____ _____   _____

                                           Subtotal   _____

                    Illinois residents add 8.75 % Sales Tax   _____

S / H Book Rate, add $2.00 for the 1st book, $1.00 for each additional   _____

                    The charge for UPS Ground is $3.50 per book   _____

                                           Grand Total   _____

International Publishing Corp., 625 N. Michigan, Suite 1920, Chicago, IL 60611